Christopher Catherwood worked as consultant to the Blair cabinet's Strategy Unit, in the Admiralty building where Churchill was based (1939–40) as First Lord of the Admiralty. He teaches history part-time at the universities of Cambridge and Richmond (Virginia), where he is annual Writer in Residence. His books include *Winston's Folly*, *Why the Nations Rage: Killing in the Name of God*, *Britain's Balkan Dilemma in World War II* and *Christians, Muslims and Islamic Rage.*

Also by Christopher Catherwood

Winston Churchill: The Flawed Genius of WWII (2009)
Five Leading Reformers: Lives at a Watershed of History (2008)
Making War in the Name of God (2007)
A Brief History of the Middle East (2006)
Winston's Folly (2004) (published in the United States as *Churchill's Folly: How Winston Churchill created Modern Iraq*)
Christians, Muslims and Islamic Rage: What is going on and why it happened (2003)
Britain's Balkan Dilemma in World War II: Britain's Balkan Dilemma 1939–41 (2003)
Why the Nations Rage: Killing in the Name of God (2002)

HIS FINEST HOUR

CHRISTOPHER
CATHERWOOD

A Herman Graf Book
Skyhorse Publishing

Skyhorse Publishing books may be purchased in bulk at special discounts for sales promotion, corporate gifts, fund-raising, or educational purposes. Special editions can also be created to specifications. For details, contact the Special Sales Department, Skyhorse Publishing, 555 Eighth Avenue, Suite 903, New York, NY 10018 or info@skyhorsepublishing.com.

www.skyhorsepublishing.com

10 9 8 7 6 5 4 3 2 1

Library of Congress Cataloging-in-Publication Data available on file

Typeset by TW Typesetting, Plymouth, Devon
Printed in the EU

To the Archives Staff
of
the Churchill Archives Centre
of
Churchill College Cambridge
who have helped countless historians over many years
with such friendship, enthusiasm and expertise
and who have done so much to make this book
and many of my other works
not just possible but such a pleasure to write.
AND
To my very favourite former Archivist
(from another collection, in the United States),
whom having met a mutual friend in those archives years
ago led him and his wife to introduce me to my wife,
Paulette with whom I have enjoyed the happiness that
Winston enjoyed with his Clementine.

CONTENTS

CONTENTS

ACKNOWLEDGMENTS

Introduction

ACKNOWLEDGEMENTS

How many acknowledgements have we read that end with something like, 'And finally I give warmest thanks to Ermintrude, who was so kind during the writing of this book . . .'

This is the biography of a happily married man. (Well, he certainly was – and apart from one possible wobble in the 1930s, one can say that Clementine was too, even though Churchill must have been an extraordinarily difficult man with whom to live, as we shall see.)

Thankfully, I am also singularly blessed in being married to a truly wonderful woman, my wife Paulette, and so perhaps it is fitting in a biography such as this to *start* the acknowledgements with her, rather than dismissing her in a few words at the end. Although I had written books before marriage to her, my real writing career coincides with marrying Paulette, and without her steadfast love, encouragement, wisdom, counsel, support and much else besides, none of the books I have written these past many years since our wedding date might ever have seen the light of day, this one fully included. So to Paulette: profounder thanks than words can ever say.

Thank you too to that publisher *par excellence* Nick Robinson, for whose Constable & Robinson imprint this is my third book. In days when so many of the older publishers have been absorbed into vast, anonymous international conglomerates – as I was writing this book I read the sad story of a centuries-old publisher whose authors began with Byron and Jane Austen, via Charles Darwin down to John Betjeman, that is now part of such a conglomerate – Constable & Robinson has managed to stay independent and keep publishing the way it used to be. Four cheers for such people, and warmest gratitude too to so many of the Constable staff, starting with my editor Leo Hollis, who kindly commissioned this book, and who is a distinguished author in his own right. His editing of the book has been a delight. Thanks, too, to Jaqueline Mitchell for her conscientious copyediting. Next we have the much appreciated and widely revered former sales director Andrew Hayward, and last but not least, the splendid East Anglia sales representative Phil Robey, who has sold so many copies of my previous books into numerous bookshops around the country, and his wife Catherine, who maintains the business.

Historians around the world have been grateful beyond measure to the staff of the Archives Centre at Churchill College here in Cambridge. Often they are unsung, which is why some of us, including Nigel Knight, have taken to thanking *all* of them, from the Director, Allen Packwood (of whom it is said if you spell his first name right you *must* be one of the *cognoscenti*) downwards. For this book, since it is on Winston

Churchill, I thought I would take it a step further and dedicate the book to them. All of them deserve it – they do a magnificent and sadly often unrecognized job, to the highest standards. They are, each one, a role model to archivists around the world on how such places should be run.

Allen Packwood, the Director, does a splendid job not just in helping historians like me – which he does superbly – but also in putting the Archives on the international map, especially in the United States, where his contacts and range of friends and supporters are prodigious, something which has done not only immense good for the Churchill Archives but also for the cause of historical research in general. Historians everywhere are grateful to Allen and I am happy to be among them.

I am equally grateful to his colleagues Andrew Riley (famous on television and beyond as the expert on the Thatcher archives, which are also in Churchill College), Natalie Adams, Katherine Thompson, Madelin Terrazas, and Sophie Bridges – whom I have been glad to get to know along with her equally delightful partner, Patrick, and who is the authority on the papers of Quintin Hogg, winner of the famous 1938 Oxford by-election.

The assistants, the main interface with the general public, have been excellent in helping with arcane technical matters such as how to use a spool, as well as fetching interminable amounts of the archive for me: Dr Lynsey Robertson (a distinguished medievalist in her own right) and, especially, Caroline Herbert, who manages a full-time job helping historians as well as being (along with her astronomer husband Peter) active in one of Cambridge's exciting new church developments. Thank you too to former staff members Claire Knight and Sandra Marsh. The conservator, Sarah Lewery – the lady in the white coat – has done a wonderful job of keeping the archives in a state in which they can still be seen, ably helped by her assistant Bridget Warrington and, last but not least, Julie Sanderson.

The archivists all live up to their reputation of being highly knowledgeable and equally personable: the administrator, legendary in the academic sphere, has excelled in keeping absent-minded historians and archivists connected to the real world. Many of the staff also eat at the College – the dining hall, in memory of Winston Churchill, is the biggest in Cambridge – and they have been the very best of lunchtime companions. The staff of the Archives Centre have become friends as well as colleagues, and I have been blessed in having such a delightful crew of people with whom to work during the research and writing of this book.

In addition, the Roskill Library is in itself a treasure trove, with books on Churchill and on the war all together in one place, whereas in a major university research library they would be spread over many floors and different rooms. The library also has American books not otherwise available in Britain, and all these factors combine together to make it a splendid resource for historians.

As I was writing this book, Churchill College – founded with the hope it would be a British version of MIT in the other Cambridge across the Atlantic – finally recognized the epic achievement of Churchill's official biographer, Sir Martin Gilbert, by making him an Honorary Fellow. It was great to be present for his speech following his election, and to see that tribute made forty years after his initial appointment; and well done from all historians to Allen Packwood in making this possible.

I was still an Archive By-Fellow of the College when I began this book; I am now an Associate of the Senior Combination Room. I am most grateful to the two distinguished scientists who made this possible: Professor Archie Howie, the SCR President, and the astronomer Dr Christopher Tout, whose ability in explaining helioseismology to an historian like me must be some kind of record! SCRs in Oxford and Cambridge colleges are by definition multi-disciplinary and it has been a great privilege to have coffee with people from so many parts of the academic spectrum, and, in Churchill's case, from so many different parts of the globe. Special thanks, too, go to my successor as Archives By-Fellow, Dr Graham Farmelo, author of the deservedly bestselling book on the physicist Paul Dirac, for encouraging me as we shared a table in the Roskill Library during the writing of this book.

I also have the great pleasure of being a Dining Member of St Edmund's College, a wonderfully cosmopolitan place in itself, and of having links with that college for more than fifteen years. Warmest thanks as in so many previous books to the countless friends from the SCR there. This is a convivial place where people are expected to – and enjoy – talking to each other, and I thank all the usual regulars whose company has proved such fun over these many years past.

I am also a Key Supervisor at Homerton College, now a full part of the university, and here warmest thanks go to Dr Steve Watts, whose regular supply of excellent students to teach, as well as his own company and that of Homerton SCR, has been such a boon since my happy association with Homerton began. Thanks too to Richard Toye, formerly of Homerton, now of Exeter University, and a distinguished scholar both on Churchill and on British twentieth-century history.

I also have the wonderful opportunity to teach for the INSTEP programme in Cambridge. Started a long while back by some academics from the LSE in London, its Cambridge branch draws each semester marvellous students from, among other places, Wake Forest, Tulane, Villanova, Hampden-Sydney and other similar well-known American institutions, who want to spend a short time studying on this side of the Atlantic. Thousands of students have been grateful to the stalwarts of the Cambridge programme Professor Geoffrey Lee Williams and his wife Janice, who are two of the most delightful people in Cambridge and an excellent couple for whom to work. (Geoffrey is still going strong and teaching aged seventy-nine. Working for someone still *that* enthusiastic is a joy in itself).

Normally I write large parts of my books at the University of Richmond, in Richmond, VA. This year I took a sabbatical from that, but I could not write these acknowledgments without giving warmest thanks to so many kind and helpful people at that splendid institution, not least to Professor John Gordon, for whose class on Churchill I was able to teach one year, and to its bookstore, whose staff have sold many copies of my works on Churchill and more besides. I was also able in 2009 to give a lecture on CSPAN Book TV at the university, and warmest thanks go to all those who made this happy event possible.

I am also grateful to the wonderful folk at the George C. Marshall Center at the Virginia Military Institute in Lexington, Virginia (my wife's old home town) for transforming my view of the Second World War, especially on the key role in winning it played by Marshall himself, the US Army Chief of Staff during that conflict. They have been southern hospitality personified. Special thanks go to Brian Shaw, Paul Barron and Ann Wells for making my research there possible, and to Mike and Lucy Wilkins for their kindness.

Many thanks too to the legendary Richard Reynolds of Heffers in Cambridge. Richard is a byword among the book trade, a chairman and much sought after member of numerous prestigious prize panels, and also the person who did the enormous favour of introducing me to Constable & Robinson at a London Book Fair a few years back. Richard and his wife Sally are famous in Cambridge for their generous hospitality, countless acts of kindness and much more besides. The first book I dedicated to Richard and Sally turned out also to be my first international success (and I have been tempted therefore to dedicate *all* my books to them in similar hope thereafter) and the encouragement the two of them have given to everything I write is second only to that of my wife and parents.

Which leads me to add that this is the first book not written at the wonderful home eleven miles out of Cambridge that my parents owned for nearly half a century, until they sold it in 2008. It was a fifteenth-century based house, and ideal for writing: well over sixty or maybe even more than seventy books by different members of the family must have been happily written there over those lyrical decades. But even though where my parents now live is smaller, my gratitude to them for their continued, splendid, loyal and enthusiastic moral support remains undiminished.

My wife and I have no children but we do have god-daughters: to them and to their families, warmest possible thanks for your friendship, kindness and personal encouragement.

Thanks, too, to Alexander McCall Smith, the novelist, for being so wonderfully helpful with my first major book for Constable, by choosing it for his book of the year in the *Mail on Sunday* back in 2004 (and giving a similar mention to the American edition in the *New York Times*), and, in 2008, being kind enough to make me a cameo character in his online novel *Corduroy Mansions*, in which I appear in Chapter 66. He is living proof that great men always have time to help others and to give, in his case, a fellow writer the time of day.

Thinking of great authors who are kind, warmest possible thanks also to four internationally distinguished historians who always take the time to be generous, informative and friendly to those, like me, who are less well-known writers: Professor Paul Kennedy of Yale University, Professor Richard Holmes of Cranfield University, Professor John Charmley of the University of East Anglia (my PhD supervisor on Churchill's creation of Iraq in 1921) and Professor Christopher Andrew here in Cambridge. Each of these academics is helpfulness personified and I am more than grateful to them all. (Thanks too to Richard's colleague, the renowned espionage and Renaissance historian Hugh Bicheno, also a Churchill expert.)

Finally, as always, the ideas and angles I take in this book are my own – on a subject such as this one, that is necessary to say, since the four gentlemen just mentioned do not, as historical biography enthusiasts will know, agree with each other – as are any blunders that have slipped through.

Christopher Catherwood
Cambridge, England
August 2009

INTRODUCTION

Winston Churchill is one of the great perennials of British and indeed world history, someone who continues to be an icon on both sides of the Atlantic. His iconic and lasting real claim to fame is based upon his leadership of Britain in the crucial years of 1940–1, without which that country would certainly have lost the war, with all the hideous consequences that would surely have flowed from such a defeat. This is why this book breaks with chronology and starts the narrative with how Churchill saved Britain – and thus probably also the Western world as well – from defeat by Hitler in 1940.

In saving Britain in 1940, rather than doing a deal with Hitler, Churchill was both morally and politically right. But this book will also show that there was a great deal more to Churchill than his finest hours in the 1940s.

One of the most significant, and now sadly overlooked, books on Churchill was the late Robert Rhodes James's 1970 work *Churchill: A Study in Failure*

1900–1939. In that book Robert argued that had Churchill died in 1939, he would have been seen not as the towering giant we perceive him to be today but as a failure – a magnificent one, perhaps, but a failure nonetheless. Although this study does not agree with Rhodes James's thesis I do want to argue several things.

Firstly, Churchill was absolutely right in taking his stance in 1940, and we are thus completely correct in regarding him as a major hero, certainly, as a BBC poll a few years ago put it, one of the very greatest Britons of all time.

But, secondly, we need to see him in proper perspective – he was, after all, someone with a unique sixty-four-year career in British politics. This means remembering what preceded the valiant years 1940–1. Just to take one example: his creation of Iraq in 1921, an entirely artificial state, still has consequences for us today in the twenty-first century. Many similar instances will become clear.

Thirdly, even in war, he did not get everything right.

Fourthly, we should never forget that he was out of office in 1931–9 not because of his staunch opposition to the disastrous policy of appeasement, but, in the main, for quite different reasons, such as his zealous and wholly reactionary opposition to even a limited form of independence for India.

In addition, before 1939, while Winston Churchill was seen with good cause as a somewhat erratic adventurer, he was, certainly in comparison with today's politicians, a major global figure who had achieved considerable success in other fields, most notably as a writer and historian.

Finally, while Churchill is today idolized on the political right (especially in the United States), we need to remember that from 1905–14 he was a leading member of one of the most successful radical governments in British history, and could be seen during that period as a leading progressive, rather than conservative, statesman.

There is a good deal more to Churchill than simply his heroic resistance to Nazi Germany. He is a far more interesting figure than either his hagiographers or denigrators allow.

So what we have here is what can best be described as a nuanced or properly balanced biography of Winston Churchill, one that fully recognizes his uniqueness, genius, triumph in rescuing Britain in 1940, yet at the same time is very open to his many faults, bad decisions and often highly erratic behaviour. Therefore, on the one hand this is not a hagiography, admitting to no mistakes by our hero, but nor is it a hatchet job, finding faults for the sake of demolishing the reputation of a national icon, and doing so for the sake of it.

In other words, both sides of the debate on Churchill have reason on their side. He really was a larger than life figure, far more so than the comparatively minor figures we see in politics today. Yet he could also be a stubborn reactionary, a loose cannon, an adventurer, whose mistakes probably ended up costing millions of lives.

Thankfully, the days of thoughtless hagiography on the one hand and mean prejudice on the other are over. Having said that, ordinary fans of Churchill still insist he was 101 per cent right 102 per cent of the time, and that any word uttered against him is blasphemy. Torrents of personal abuse still rain down upon those who argue that Churchill was only 99 per cent perfect, and a historian has to learn to develop a thick skin. But when it comes to serious history, there are excellent writers on both sides of the divide, as the bibliography will explain.

Finally, this is a *'Brief'* biography, not a full-length and definitive work. It does not pretend to match the encyclopaedic quality of the Martin Gilbert volumes, or the size and scope, for example, of the biography of Churchill by another famous British politician, Roy Jenkins. It is, if you like, a starter course, to whet the appetite for those who want to discover the basics about Winston Churchill before they go on to read much longer works covering in more detail particular aspects of Churchill's very full and adventurous nine decades.

I

HIS FINEST HOUR

Churchill's fame rests upon his heroic years as Prime Minister and Minister of Defence in the Second World War, from 1939–45. In particular, he kept Britain going in the crucial period May 1940 to December 1941, when America entered the conflict, and Britain was, as Churchill understood, safe at last.

In retrospect, victory seems obvious. But it was far from feeling like that at the time, and many is the occasion when Britain could have fallen to Nazi domination. While the nation's geographical island status and the staunch bravery of the armed services and of the people themselves – especially during the Blitz – certainly helped, one of the major reasons why the country survived is that its Prime Minister was Winston Churchill, someone whose whole life seemed to have been in readiness for just such a time of trial.

We have probably all heard at least parts of the speech

that Churchill, also Minister of Defence, made to the House of Commons on 13 May 1940, the speech that the editor of his collected speeches, Sir Robert Rhodes James, has rightly described as 'one of the most crucial in modern history':

> I have nothing to offer but blood, toil, tears and sweat. We have before us an ordeal of the most grievous kind. We have before us many long months of struggle and suffering. You ask, what is our policy? I can say: It is to wage war by sea, land and air, with all our might and with all the strength that God can give us; to wage war against a monstrous tyranny, never surpassed in the dark, lamentable catalogue of human crime. That is our policy. You ask, what is our aim? I can answer in one word: It is *victory*, victory at all costs, victory in spite of all terror, victory however long and hard the road may be; for without victory there is no survival.

Nowadays, post-Obama victory, we are beginning again to lose the cynicism of the past few decades and once more to appreciate the power of stirring oratory such as this, perhaps because such ways of speaking have been devalued in the intervening six decades. This is *truly* wonderful material, yet people at the time would not have heard this speech *live* – they would only have heard subsequent radio broadcasts, as Parliament was not recorded until over thirty years later. But many contemporaries *felt* they had heard him, and that is just as important. By way of light relief, Churchill saw his personal advisor Desmond Morton just after making the speech and, almost tearful by then, told him, 'That got the sods, didn't it . . .'. For, as we forget, Churchill was still, if anything, more popular on the Labour and Liberal benches than his own. However electric the atmosphere in retrospect for us, that is not how many in the 'establishment' saw it at the time: Lord Halifax, the Foreign Secretary, would have been their choice to lead the country, with all the doleful consequences that might have followed, including surrender to Germany by the end of the year.

In May 1940, oratory was about all Churchill possessed with which to defeat Hitler. Conscription was not fully operative, and the tiny British army was still in a parlous state. Here I think the former Keeper of the Churchill Archives, Piers Brendon, makes a good point: it was not Churchill who changed in May 1940, on becoming Prime Minister, but the British people themselves. Churchill, as his biographers are right to point out, was truly a warrior, not a former Lord Mayor with an umbrella, as Neville Chamberlain had been. The British people felt that here was a man to lead them through thick and thin, and, as we shall see, until the end of 1942 there was far more of the thin than of the thick. Survivors of 1940 do not forget this, though, nor the frighteningly small margin by which Britain survived conquest.

In the next two years Churchill was to make many mistakes, which need not be disguised. In some cases they were potentially disastrous and British independence from Hitler hung by the narrowest of threads right through to 1941. But there was one thing that Churchill got supremely right, and that is something that most British biographers have underestimated. Churchill, a half-American himself, knew that without the United States, the United Kingdom and British Empire were finished. Only by America's entry into the war could Britain ever hope to defeat the Third Reich, Japan and Italy. Otherwise, the British could perhaps hang on, however slenderly, but actually to defeat the Axis would remain an impossible demand. All this Churchill understood, and his ability to keep Britain afloat and unconquered until the United States entered the war in 1941 was perhaps his finest achievement of all.

As for the idea that he should have parleyed with Hitler, perhaps through a still-neutral Mussolini, surely this notion should be deemed morally unacceptable, let alone historically crazy? Yet even serious historians have pondered it, alas . . . But while Halifax as Prime Minister, or a continuing Neville Chamberlain, might have entertained such barbaric and defeatist notions, Churchill rightly rejected them.

Churchill believed in the age-old British tradition of fighting wars with continental Allies. Unfortunately for him – and for the French people – France in 1940 was a deeply troubled country, whose military and political command structure was highly fragile. Accounts of exactly *why* France fell so swiftly to the Germans, once war on the Western Front was finally joined after months of Phoney War, are many and various, and usually in disagreement with each other.

Suffice it to say that Churchill did his very best to fill the French leadership with resolve, but, in the end, the tiny British Expeditionary Force (BEF), together with the supposed might of the once great French army, proved utterly incapable of outwitting and outmanoeuvring the sheer power and strategic brilliance of the *Wehrmacht*, now at the height of its martial prowess. It was only a tactical blunder by Hitler that allowed the BEF, and many French troops, to make their miraculous escape from Dunkirk at all. Much vitally needed British equipment had to be left behind, and many a British soldier was to spend the rest of the conflict as a German prisoner of war.

With France fallen, Britain was now very alone in Europe. This period has gone down in British national folklore, and Churchill was to give this period the name of 'finest hour'. And with victory inevitable after Pearl Harbor, it is easy to forget that slim margin for survival. Churchill himself did not take it at all for granted, and this is why he set about doing everything possible to make sure that Britain was able to hang on until his great dream of American intervention turned out to be true.

Churchill's most famous and defiant wartime speech was delivered to the House of Commons on 4 June 1940, and is revered for what are, in fact, only its last few lines. One can easily understand the great American journalist and Anglophile Edward R. Morrow (best known in the United States for his opposition to McCarthy in the 1950s, but loved in Britain for telling the American people how England survived the Blitz) when he said later that Churchill mobilized the English language and turned it into an instrument of war.

> Even though large tracts of Europe and many old and famous states have fallen or may fall into the grip of the Gestapo and all the odious apparatus of Nazi rule, we shall not flag or fail. We shall go on to the end, we shall

> fight in France, we shall fight on the seas and oceans, we shall fight with growing confidence and growing strength in the air, we shall defend our Island, whatever the cost may be, we shall fight on the beaches, we shall fight on the landing grounds, we shall fight in the fields and in the streets, we shall fight in the hills; we shall never surrender . . .

Not many people know an unofficial part of this speech that, during the cheers, Churchill whispered to his new deputy, the Labour Leader Clement Attlee: 'We'll fight them with the butt end of broken beer bottles because that's all we've bloody got . . .'.

How true that last statement was! One of the most enduringly popular television shows in Britain in the past forty years has been *Dad's Army*, a now oft-repeated series of how a group of Home Guard volunteers meet each week in the fictional town of Walmington-on-Sea to drill and practice against a German invasion that thankfully never comes. The part-time soldiers certainly had enthusiasm and patriotic zeal, in real life as well as in drama, but how brave but incredibly amateur fighters would have survived with pitchforks and little else against the combined might of the *Wehrmacht* and *Luftwaffe* if it had ever come is a question to which one can be glad that we shall never need to know the answer. There is little doubt that most of them would have fought in hills, beaches, fields and streets, but the likelihood that many of the now smaller British Army would have survived is alas slender.

In fact Churchill knew from where aid could come, and this is how he finished his speech that day:

> And even if we do [i.e. surrender] which I do not for a moment believe, [and] this Island or a large part of it were subjugated and starving, then our Empire beyond the seas, armed and guarded by the British Fleet, would carry on the struggle, until, in God's good time, the New World, with all its power and might, steps forth to the rescue and liberation of the old.

This was, of course, a monumental gamble on Churchill's part, one that had it failed would have left Britain ruined and almost certainly defeated by the juggernaut of the Third Reich. The sad fact is, as historians such as Max Hastings remind us, that the Army had been so run down throughout the 1930s, there simply had not been the time to bring it fully back up to scratch and to full fighting order. The rebuilding of the Army got going when war began, but mid-1940 was just a few months into this critical process, and before aid from the United States had really got going effectively.

As Churchill told the British people in a broadcast on 17 June 1940:

> The news from France is very bad . . . We have become the sole champions now in arms to defend the world cause . . . We shall defend our Island home, and with the British Empire we shall fight on unconquerable until the curse of Hitler is lifted from the brows of mankind. We are sure that in the end all will come right.

All did come right but it was to be far closer than the British people knew. Nor was Britain totally alone, as many Canadians, Australians and New Zealanders can bear witness and as Churchill reminded the House of

Commons in his 'Finest Hour' speech, in which he ended by saying:

> I expect that the Battle of Britain is about to begin. Upon this battle depends the survival of Christian civilization. Upon it depends our own British life, and the long continuity of our institutions and our Empire. The whole fury and might of the enemy must very soon be turned upon us. Hitler knows that he will have to break us in this Island or lose the war . . . if we fail, then the whole world, including the United States, including all that we have known and cared for, will sink into the abyss of a new Dark Age made more sinister, and perhaps more protracted, by the lights of perverted science. Let us therefore brace ourselves to our duties, and so bear ourselves that, if the British Empire and its Commonwealth last for a thousand years, men will still say, 'This was their finest hour'.

Churchill was not exaggerating. If the Nazis had ruled from the Atlantic to the Pacific, which they could have done had Britain fallen, then the consequences for the future of the world would have been every bit as hideous as Churchill proclaimed. This is also important in the light of comment by revisionists that Britain should have done a deal with Hitler and let him attack the Soviet Union. The Third Reich would then have stretched from Calais to Vladivostok, with the most horrific results imaginable. Not only that, but how on earth could Britain have maintained any genuine independence from so vast a behemoth? The idea is surely untenable. Churchill was right: the very existence of Western democratic civilization truly was at stake.

Today Churchill is the great British bull-dog. But in his early days as Prime Minister it was still Chamberlain who was cheered by the Conservatives from the backbenches in the House of Commons. Chamberlain was well treated by his successor, who allowed him to stay on for a while in Downing Street, and in the Cabinet itself. However, he died in the autumn, with Churchill elected to succeed him as Leader of the Conservative Party in October 1940, an event that would surely not have taken place but for the war. Thus Churchill was free to set his own course. He squeezed Lord Halifax out of the Cabinet as Foreign Secretary, sending him thousands of miles away to Washington DC as British Ambassador to the United States, a fairly titular post since Churchill and Roosevelt contacted each other directly henceforth during the war. (The pro-Nazi Duke of Windsor was similarly exiled as Governor of Bermuda.)

Churchill now had a proper Coalition government, with at least two members of the Labour Party in the small War Cabinet (the group of around five or so politicians at the head of the government), fellow Conservative Anthony Eden back at the Foreign Office, and the Trade Union boss Ernest Bevin in the vital economic post of Minister of Labour.

In the short term, perhaps the most important appointment he made was of his Canadian friend, the press baron Lord Beaverbrook, as Minister of Aircraft Production. During the 1930s the Government had concentrated – some would say foolishly – on building bombers. Now, with the Luftwaffe flying daily over British skies in what became known as the Battle of Britain, what were needed were fighters, to prevent enemy incursion. Since Britain was an island, Germany needed air superiority over British skies before launching its invasion plan, *Operation Sea Lion*.

Beaverbrook was able to mobilize British resources not merely to manufacture enough fighters, but also to reconstruct many that were damaged but not altogether destroyed during the Battle itself. This, along with the exceptional strategic genius of Air Chief Marshal Dowding of the Royal Air Force (RAF), managed to turn the tide – but only *just*. By the narrowest of margins, the RAF fighters (now including a large Polish contingent, and some brave American Eagle Squadron pilots) were able to defeat the Luftwaffe over the skies of Britain and preserve the country from the invasion that would otherwise have inevitably followed.

During this period Churchill went to the headquarters of 11 Group Fighter Command, in Uxbridge, a western suburb of London. The 15 September 1940 saw one of the largest Luftwaffe raids on London, a day Churchill had chosen for one of his visits. When he arrived, every single light bulb that designated a fighter group was on. He asked the Group Controller, 'All your forces are in the air. What do we do now?'

The Controller, who knew how dire the situation was, replied, 'Well sir, we can just hope that the squadrons will refuel as quickly as possible and get up again.' *All of them were in the air . . .*

Soon more German incoming aircraft were spotted. 'What other reserves do we have?' asked an anxious Prime Minister.

There were no reserves that night – they were *all* in the air . . .

With just a hair's breadth, Britain had enough fighters finally to defeat the Luftwaffe over British skies, and within two days of Churchill's visit, the crisis was over. The Battle of Britain had been won. Britain was safe – but while we know now that the invasion would never happen, we must recall that they did not know that then, and real fear of a German attack remained for some years to come.

Furthermore, Hitler made what many have judged to be the strategic mistake of then switching to bombing cities instead of airbases, starting with London. This period, known in Britain as the Blitz, short for the German *blitzkrieg* or 'lightning war', saw 43,000 civilians killed, more than 139,000 wounded and 2.5 million made homeless. Throughout this entire period, Churchill remained indomitable, regularly visiting bombed out parts of London, his sheer physical presence, as much as anything he said, giving him his 'bull-dog image' of defiance and perseverance when all else around seemed to be falling. He was often in London even during the worst of the Blitz – as was the royal family – and that in itself inspired the reputation that has lasted ever since, in the eyes of ordinary people; cries of 'Good Old Winnie' were as much about his spirit as his leadership.

However, as contemporary diaries reveal, Churchill was not trusted at all by what we now call the 'establishment' (a term coined in the 1950s), and many of the civil service and Conservative Party grandees continued strongly to distrust him for quite some while. These were not just the old appeasers – though those such as R.A. Butler certainly did not hide their distaste for Churchill and his raffish friends – but much of what some historians have called the 'Respectable Tendency' in British politics and in the wider echelons of upper class society, including those such as Jock Colville, one of Chamberlain's and then Churchill's Private Secretaries in Downing Street, who were later to be fully converted to the Churchillian cause.

In his memoirs, Churchill gives the impression of a strongly united government, determined, as he so eloquently put it, to resist Hitler at all costs. However, the wartime archives reveal a vast discrepancy between what *actually happened* and *what Churchill said happened later on.* It took quite some while for Churchill to be in *real* command of his own government, and in 1940 there was much internal debate within the Coalition as to what Britain should do, with the old appeasers, such as Halifax and Butler, still pressing for a negotiated surrender. Churchill is thus quite misleading to say later on that he never gave it the remotest consideration. In fact, the situation in 1940 was so bad that it *had* to be discussed, if only to be rejected. However, this was the moment when Churchill reminded the War Cabinet that 'nations which went down fighting rose again, but those who surrendered tamely were finished.' He went on to tell other members of the Government that, 'If this long island story of ours is to end at last, let it end only when each one of us lies choking in his own blood upon the ground.' He told his personal Chief of Staff, General Sir Hastings Ismay, that he would prefer to die fighting.

There is a saying that it is better to be a general later on in a war, when your side is winning, than at the beginning, when your armies are close to defeat. If ever that were true, it was so with the British Army in the Second World War. The early British Generals – Gort, Ironside and the one that the Americans liked the most, Dill – were not great warriors. On top of that, in Churchill, who was now Minister of Defence as well as Prime Minister, the Armed Services had a political overlord whose tendency to micromanage everything, down to the last battleship and regiment deployment, was to drive to despair all those who had to work with him.

Being Minister of Defence was a wise move by Churchill. There was then no Ministry of Defence proper – the full-scale department did not exist as it does now until 1964 – but Churchill had his own senior staff officer, General Sir Hastings Ismay (called 'Pug' because of his canine expression), who acted as the liaison between the Minister of Defence and the three separate Chiefs of Staff of the individual services: the Chief of the Imperial General Staff (for the Army (CIGS)), the First Sea Lord (for the Admiralty) and the Chief of Air Staff (for the RAF).

In theory the three were equals, which did not help, since inter-service rivalry was not at all diminished by the advent of war. But in practice, after Sir Alan Brooke (later Lord Alanbrooke) became CIGS in 1941, he acted as the de facto senior member of the Chiefs of Staff Committee, and as the unofficial shop steward of the three services in their dealings with their political boss. Both Churchill and Brooke were, however, very much part of the British military consensus on how to wage war against an enemy on the European continent, one that went back centuries, in a way that could not be said so much of the United States, for which the kind of total war now being waged was something with which it had become familiar only since the Civil War. It is this cultural clash that, as the conflict developed, led to the differences in strategy on how to win the war that emerged between the two Western allies.

Sir John Dill, Brooke's predecessor and Churchill's initial CIGS, was someone who provoked the worst kind of bullying and wrath in the Prime Minister, to whom this distinguished soldier was no more than 'Dilly-dally'. As Sir Alan Brooke confided to his wartime diary, 'I shall never be able to forgive Winston for his attitude towards Dill', a sentiment that the Americans, notably their Army Chief of Staff General George C. Marshall, were fully to share.

The other senior commander to feel the lash of Churchill's ire was Sir Archibald Wavell, who remains one of the most discussed and written about generals of the Second World War, since, in order to get rid of him from the field, Churchill made him Viceroy of India, and thus responsible for much of the debacle in the sub-continent, as independence continued to be denied while Churchill was Prime Minister.

Wavell was a strange mix of the taciturn and artistic – he was an expert on poetry. But mainly he was unlucky, and lacked the Marlborough-like dash, confidence and verve that Churchill demanded from his commanders. And, as we shall soon see, both Wavell and Dill were to be implicated in one of the most catastrophic British strategic decisions of the Second World War.

Brooke always said of Churchill that the Prime Minister kept on coming up with ludicrous ideas – the classic one being the idea of invading Norway, Operation *Jupiter* – and that it was his job as CIGS to prevent them. Churchill, however, never *completely* over-ruled his commanders, unlike Hitler, who did so frequently, and with such ultimately devastating and terminal consequences. Nevertheless, while this is true, to an extent, it did not stop Churchill from going regularly to the brink, right down to battalion level, as his voluminous wartime correspondence shows.

Above all, Churchill wanted *action*, and lots of it. In this, of course, he had very good reason, for the appalling lack of any kind of action during the Phoney War made the defeat of France far worse than it otherwise might have been, if it did not actually cause it, French incompetence notwithstanding. To Churchill, Britain was at war! The country had to do *something*, and after Britain survived the battle for its skies, Churchill was all for fighting Germany wherever and whenever possible.

Britain had always been primarily a naval power and what is now called the 'continental commitment' – British armies on European soil – was something that was traditionally avoided as much as possible. But when France fell, Churchill found himself with an entirely new problem. As we know, the United Kingdom had always fought in conjunction with *allies* – Marlborough with the Dutch, Wellington with the Prussians. In the First World War, Britain's great continental ally was France. However, now, with the Nazi conquest, that ally was no longer available. Indeed, in June 1940 Britain and its Empire had no real continental allies at all, especially one of any proper military significance. Britain truly was, in the *European* sense, incredibly alone.

So Churchill adopted the other strategy of years gone by, what Israeli historian Tuvia Ben-Moshe and military strategists down the centuries have termed the *peripheral* or *indirect approach*: that is, not just to go for the principal enemy head-on, but to find the weak spots of its allies, and attack them. He took the conflict to three areas:

(a) The underground attack, with which he was familiar from the Boer War, using guerrilla tactics, through the newly created Special Operations Executive (SOE);
(b) Bomber Command: hitting back directly at the enemy;
(c) North Africa – waging war on the periphery.

All these methods were controversial, but were felt by Churchill, especially after Britain was fighting alone, to be the only means of waging war successfully.

Churchill's policy of 'setting Europe ablaze', of creating an underground British force to help resistance movements, was a move fraught with dangers, not least to the local populations. While there is much glamour associated with SOE – witness the films based upon it, both those representing the reality, such as *Ill Met By Moonlight*, and those of the imagination, such as *The Guns of Navarone* and *Charlotte Gray* – the sad truth is that the atrocities wreaked in revenge by the Nazis, especially in the Balkans, far outweighed the gains.

More controversial still was Churchill's support of Bomber Command. Churchill had helped to create the Royal Air Force, and was a staunch defender of its doctrines. So too, during the war, were all three of the Chiefs of Staff, especially the Chief of Air Staff, Sir Charles Portal. In late 1940 Churchill was to tell the War Cabinet:

> The Fighters are our salvation, but the Bombers alone provide the means of victory. We must therefore develop the power to carry an ever-increasing volume of explosives to Germany, so as to pulverise the entire industry and scientific structure on which the war effort and the economic life of the enemy depend, while holding him at arm's length from our Island. In no other way at present visible can we hope to overcome the immense military power of Germany.

In fact, by waging war against the Axis in the Middle East, Churchill was to show that there was indeed another way. But the idea of bombing being a path to victory is one of the great myths of war, and one believed by both Churchill and the military establishment of the time.

Two arguments can be made, one military and the other moral, that this path was not all it was supposed to be, something that Churchill slowly began to realize for himself as the war progressed.

The moral case was made by the brave and outspoken Bishop Geoffrey Bell of Chichester, during the conflict itself. Killing soldiers was one thing, but slaughtering thousands of civilians was quite another, and, as the massive carnage of the Allied bombing of Dresden towards the end of the war shows, huge numbers of non-combatants died, often even without any strategic advantage being gained. To Bell and others, this was contrary to all the laws of war as evolved by the Church over millennia. However barbaric the Luftwaffe raids on Britain – such as that on London during the Blitz – with thousands of *British* civilian deaths, that did not justify Britain being as savage to the Germans as the Nazis were to them. Churchill did not like Bishop Bell, but he did admit privately during the war, 'Are we beasts? Are we taking this too far?'

Richard Holmes has helpfully summarized the strategic background to much of Churchill's own position, which some have argued fluctuated through the war. At the start of the conflict, bombing Germany was, like fighting in North Africa, something that the British could actually do to take the war to the Reich. Britain could not fight the Germans direct, but the RAF could bomb them, and that also gave the impression of action that everyone needed. But once other options became available, then Churchill changed his mind, especially as he realized, towards the end of the war, that a Germany that had been pulverized would be one that would be difficult to reconstruct. As Holmes reminds us, bombing had done more physical damage to that country than the entire Thirty Years' War of the seventeenth century, from which the devastated areas took decades to recover. So Churchill was ambivalent, and that is why people are never quite sure what he felt and when. Churchill therefore took what was, in many ways, an extraordinarily risky and potentially foolhardy step: he took the war against the Axis to North Africa.

Today, Britons tend to remember the good days of this part of the struggle: the wonderful morale-boosting victory in late 1942 at El Alamein, of Montgomery beating the Desert Fox, Field Marshal Rommel, and of Churchill celebrating that triumph by insisting that church bells be rung across the country. However, for most of the three years – 1940 to 1943 – it was one British disaster after another. British and Empire forces came within a hair's breadth of defeat on numerous occasions, and if the ultimate catastrophe had come, Hitler would have been able to sweep through Egypt, capture Iraq, and have all the oil of the Middle East at his disposal. Thankfully, although such a calamity came close, the British, Australian and, after 1943, American forces always managed narrowly to avert collapse.

In those years, Britain and its Empire allies were actually fighting Hitler, even if very indirectly, and certainly a long way from the Fortress Europe under Nazi rule. By 1941 British troops, under the overall command of General Wavell, and under the more immediate supervision of General Richard O'Connor, were both on the offensive and were fighting very successfully indeed against the Italian forces in North and East Africa. Ethiopia was successfully recaptured, and O'Connor's troops were within a hair's breadth of eliminating the Axis from North Africa altogether. Victory was in sight.

It was at this very moment, with military triumph around the corner, that Churchill pulled the plug and, completely unintentionally, deprived Britain of certain victory. Instead Churchill decided to divert many of the successful British, Australian and New Zealand forces from North Africa, where they were winning, to a quixotic attempt to rescue Greece from Axis invasion. This denuded O'Connor of vitally needed reinforcements, and, as a result, the German Panzer divisions under their commander, Marshal Rommel, were able to land in North Africa.

Rommel proved an able foe, and it was not to be until well into 1943, two crucial years later, that the Allies, now with American aid, were able finally to expel the Axis from North Africa, and concentrate on the main war against Hitler, in Europe.

Britain therefore snatched defeat out of the jaws of victory, and thus we have all heard of Montgomery, who won in 1942, but not of O'Connor, the general who came within an inch of sweeping the Axis out of Africa altogether in 1941, but who then had to see all his gains lost; and, on top of that, had the supreme bad luck to be captured by the enemy and spend much of the next few years as a prisoner of war. Not only that, but in the fall of the Greek mainland to the Axis, and then the island of Crete, Britain had to suffer another defeat, as John Keegan has put it, 'a second Dunkirk', with thousands of troops captured and large amounts of invaluable military material falling into enemy hands. Churchill's Greek campaign was a total disaster whichever way one looks at it.

There is, however, one canard: namely, that as Hitler had to invade the Balkans in 1941, to help out Mussolini (whose attempt to conquer Greece unaided had turned into pure fiasco), Operation *Barbarossa*, the German invasion of the Soviet Union, was crucially delayed, and that in a way resulted in the failure of the *Wehrmacht* to conquer Russia, since by the time in 1941 they reached Moscow it had turned to winter.

Had this been true, then even disaster in Greece, as well as the Axis conquest of neighbouring Yugoslavia, was not in vain, since it prevented the far worse catastrophe of the successful conquest of the USSR.

However, recent research has backed up the reminiscences of British generals writing back in the 1950s that showed that this is all a myth: in truth, the delay of *Barbarossa* was in fact purely weather-related, and the need for Hitler to divert some of his divisions to the Balkans would in reality have made no difference at all. Churchill's reasoning in moving Allied forces to rescue Greece (and thus divert Nazi troops) therefore proves invalid, according to this reckoning; quite apart from the fact that although the Soviets came close to defeat in 1941, it is arguable that no invasion of Russia from the west ever succeeds, as Napoleon also found to his cost.

However, from 1940–1 there was one thing that Churchill understood supremely and rightly, and which made *the* crucial difference to British survival. Churchill knew that if the United States came in on the British side, then, as the Welsh writer and preacher Martyn Lloyd-Jones predicted correctly back in 1941, Britain would be safe. Very few British politicians understood the vital importance of the United States, but Churchill was one of them. He was also an imperialist to his core, and this makes his understanding of America all the more impressive, since Empire loyalists usually ignored the United States, as Chamberlain and his kind so foolishly did.

Churchill wooed Roosevelt as soon as it was possible (we can now read the entire correspondence, and it makes for fascinating study). For by 1941 the nightmare of the pre-war Chiefs of Staff had come true: Britain was at war with Germany, Italy and Japan *simultaneously*, the one eventuality that all the armed services pre-1939 had argued should never happen, because Britain simply would not be able to cope. In one sense they were right, and as one defeat followed another, it was clear that Britain hung on by its fingernails. Had Britain had to face all this on its own (albeit including the Dominions, such as Canada and Australia), it is possible that it would have lost the war by attrition. In 1942, for example, Tobruk was to fall in North Africa and Singapore was conquered by the Japanese. Had the United States not been in the war on Britain's side by this time, things could – and probably would – have been far worse still.

2

SURVIVING CHILDHOOD

Sad childhoods can be a blight on both rich and poor, along with parental neglect and similar misfortunes. This, alas, was true even of Winston Churchill. So let us look at his immediate background, and his family, before delving into the sources of his famous and often-described childhood sorrow.

Much is well known about Churchill's upbringing. He was the elder son of Lord Randolph Churchill, a younger son of the Duke of Marlborough and the owner of Blenheim Palace, near Oxford. The first Duke of Marlborough, John Churchill, was the hero of many victorious campaigns in Britain's wars in the late seventeenth and early eighteenth centuries, and as Professor Richard Holmes, a biographer of both men, has demonstrated, the first Churchill has a very legitimate claim to be regarded, along with the later Duke of Wellington, as one of the finest military leaders that Britain has ever produced.

At the time Churchill was born, in 1874, many an impecunious British and French aristocrat solved the problem of how to maintain the family estate and country mansion by marrying an American heiress. One such marriage was between Churchill's cousin and Consuelo Vanderbilt, the heiress to a vast American railroad fortune. It has been thought that Lord Randolph's marriage to New York socialite Jenny Jerome was equally opportunistic and arranged, but it now seems that this is unfair. Not only was it a genuine love match, but also Jenny, while not poor, was certainly no heiress on the Vanderbilt scale.

Being a younger son meant that Lord Randolph Churchill had to make his own way in the world. This he did through being a politician, as a Conservative. His political career could be called meteoric, since he rapidly rose to be Chancellor of the Exchequer, in charge of the nation's finances, and then threw away any hope of further advance by a badly timed resignation from office that allowed the wily Conservative leader and Prime Minister, the Marquess of Salisbury, to call his bluff. Lord Randolph went from being seen as a future Prime Minister to a fallen political has-been all in a matter of days, something from which he was never able to recover. His mysterious last illness and early death, when hardly middle-aged, sealed any chance of a comeback. Like a comet, he shone and then vanished, with a profound effect on his son.

One does not have to be a psychotherapist to understand the huge and lasting damage that a profoundly unhappy childhood can have on an individual, even through their adulthood. Back in the 1870s, the heyday of British imperial power, even the most rudimentary forms of psychology were unknown. But with hindsight there is no doubt whatsoever: Winston Leonard Spencer Churchill, born to privilege and position in the still hierarchical society of the British Empire, was a seriously neglected child. No parents could have been more selfish, uncaring or neglectful than his. That he managed to survive as well as he did, and in an age in which the psychological support mechanisms and medication that we now take for granted did not even begin to exist is the first sign of his formidable power, since he survived traumas that would have felled most of the rest of us.

Much has been said by the more critical of his biographers: that he was a monstrous egotist, over-conscious of his own genius, and a hard taskmaster who seldom took accounts of the needs of those working under his command. But while there is considerable merit in such a view, it is surely also right to say that we cannot understand the behaviour of the man unless we grasp the sheer endless trauma undergone by the child. Churchill was not merely a depressive, the condition he referred to as his 'Black Dog', something now much better grasped and treatable, but the victim of childhood neglect, which some experts have described as a form of child abuse, with all the mental lifelong scars that such treatment inflicts. In those days he had to grin and bear it; nowadays he would be on Prozac and a guest on *Oprah*.

Churchill, like many of his class, was sent away to school at a barbarically young age: at just nine years old he was at a preparatory school, St George's School in Ascot, in which beatings were far from uncommon, and in which children of the middle and upper classes could be dumped while their parents got on with their busy lives. Then such things were taken for granted – even the less privileged C.S. Lewis suffered similar horrors at his preparatory school, about which his published snippets of autobiography bear cogent witness. Today, many child psychologists would accuse such wilful parents of neglect or even maltreatment: in those days it was a burden simply to be endured.

A typical Churchill letter of this time is one he wrote in June 1884 to his mother, whom he worshipped unrequitedly from afar: 'It is very unkind of you not to write to me before this, I have had only one letter from you this term . . .'. Another, written in October 1885, this time to his father, from a crammer at which Churchill spend an interlude, also demonstrates how he felt: 'I cannot think why you did not come to see me, while you were in Brighton. I was very disappointed, but I suppose you were too busy to come.'

The lack of parental visits continued even when Churchill became a pupil at Harrow School, which, even with the transport of those days, was not exactly a great distance for his parents to come from central London. He wrote rather pathetically to his father in June 1888, 'When are you coming to see me? Please come soon and let me know by what train to meet you . . .' Needless to say, his father never came.

Churchill's time at Harrow was far from being a success. His housemaster there, the Revd J.E.C. Welldon, was constantly appalled at what he regarded as his pupils continuously 'slovenly' behaviour. Young Winston was frequently late for class, committed acts of hooliganism, and had an altogether disastrous academic record. While many of his social class progressed naturally from secondary school to Oxford or Cambridge, the best that the school could think of for him was the Army, which in those days was officered by men from the right kind of class, and not necessarily with any degree of intellectual acuity. His reports from school do not make happy reading, and this was, understandably, a source of major and perpetual sorrow and embarrassment for his parents.

Churchill's most famous letter of sorrow was written in December 1891. The previous month his despairing housemaster had suggested that Churchill spend some time learning French in Rouen – as Prime Minster during the Second World War his French accent showed how little he learned – and this caused the now sixteen-year-old Winston to get into a tower of rage, since the visit to France precluded his being able to spend meaningful time over the Christmas holidays with his family. As he wrote to his mother on 16 December 1891:

> Never would I believe that you would have been so unkind. I am utterly miserable. That you should refuse to read my letter is most painful to me . . . I am more unhappy than I could possibly say . . .

Letters like this are heart-rending. But there is an alternative view, put notably by the military historians Richard Holmes and Hugh Bicheno, which puts this correspondence in a different light, and is worth considering, since the accepted view of Churchill – the miserable child – is very much part and parcel of the Churchillian canon.

* * *

In his genuine suffering, Churchill was very typical of boys from his social class of the time, and in asking his parents to come to see him, for instance, he was requiring of them kindly behaviour that would have been unthinkable for adults then. Parents hardly ever came to visit their offspring: that was one of the points of boarding school.

Bicheno also makes another telling observation. We know of Churchill's academically-challenged and sorrowful childhood mainly through his own autobiography, *My Early Life*. Principally, as we shall soon see, this is full of his military adventures, in South Africa and in the Sudan, and, of course, it puts the author in the most heroic light possible. The timing of the book – during Churchill's so-called 'Wilderness Years' in the 1930s – is also significant. He was trying to keep himself in the public gaze, and in the most favourable way possible.

Seeing his unhappy childhood – in what twenty-first century critics refer to as misery memoirs – naturally evokes our sympathy. Poor Winston . . . And this is also what his own family does, most notably his nephew Peregrine Churchill and grand-daughter Celia Sandys in the book *From Winston With Love and Kisses*, an edited highlight of the young Winston's letters home.

Therefore, Hugh Bicheno argues, our human sympathy for Churchill, and his unhappy early days, is all part of a deliberate political ploy: lonely boy goes on to overcome all the odds and become the military hero we all know and come to love.

Thus, not only were Churchill's childhood experiences typical of his class, but the way in which he draws attention to them is integral to the creation of the

Churchillian myth that Churchill himself did so much to foster. In fact, what the letters do is not so much to give an account of unique misery, but to show how selfish he was, a trait that, alas, he was to show throughout his entire adult life as well.

There is no doubt that countless middle- and upper-class children suffered – and surely still do – because of the British elite's propensity to send their children away from home, often from as young as eight, to boarding schools miles from home. Not only that, but if one reads, for example, the autobiography of someone temperamentally very different from Churchill, the Oxford don and creator of *Narnia*, C.S. Lewis, it is evident that Churchill's suffering at barbaric preparatory schools is far from untypical. C.S. Lewis could match Winston Churchill for suffering any day, as his accounts make clear. So it is not just Churchill as an individual for whose misery we may feel sorrow, it is an entire social class.

However, while this point is well taken – most aristocratic and professional parents neglected their offspring horribly – that does not minimize the deep and lasting unhappiness that Churchill genuinely felt at his uncaring exile from home. Just because what he and C.S. Lewis underwent was common, that does not remove both the hurt at the time and the lifelong psychological scars that marked them and so many of those who suffered similar experiences, both then and since. And since many of the ruling class in his own time would also have undergone agonies as children, they would, in reading Churchill's *My Early Life*, have not responded to the story of his schooldays with anything like the degree of horrified outrage that those of us educated very differently feel today when we read such pitiful childhood letters home.

We all know that Churchill suffered from depression, and inevitably, psychologists have wanted to find out more, starting most notably in the 1960s with the distinguished Jungian psychiatrist Anthony Storr. He wrote on Churchill 'the Man' in *Churchill: Four Faces and the Man*, with the other chapters examining more standard topics such as Churchill as a strategist or politician.

As Storr correctly points out, even though he was a professional clinician:

> The psychiatrist who takes it upon himself to attempt a character study of an individual whom he has never met is engaged upon a project which is full of risk ... [especially] when considering someone who has died.

This is indeed true, however fascinating a subject Churchill's psychological makeup may be. But so important was Churchill, and so much better is our understanding today of psychology, we do at least need to give it a try.

At least one historian has speculated that Churchill suffered from Asperger's syndrome, a condition whose patients find it hard to form normal human relationships. However, as Oxford clinical psychologist Jonquil Drinkwater has suggested, the person suffering from Asperger's is the one in a circle of friends who doesn't get the joke. Churchill not only got the joke but was often the one who made it. As Drinkwater points out, however, there is not the slightest doubt that Churchill suffered badly from depression, and also made many key decisions, especially during the Second World War, while suffering from his 'Black Dog'. If, as the psychologist Anthony Storr averred back in the 1960s, Churchill had a depressive personality, this would also go some way towards explaining his treatment of his subordinates.

Storr also thinks that the form of depression from which Churchill suffered – an hereditary kind going way back to John Churchill, 1st Duke of Marlborough – had within it a strong form of narcissism, which would, one can argue, have equally as valid a claim on why he was so unfeeling to his subordinates as other conditions upon which people have speculated. Psychologists agree today that many kinds of depression are genetic – we are born with a tendency towards it – and in terms of twenty-first century clinical opinion, it makes considerable sense to see Churchill as a classic hereditary sufferer from depression in at least one form or another.

More controversially perhaps, Storr adds that Churchill never got over the 'infantile omnipotence' phase through which all babies go. Normal people, as we grow up, realize that the world does not revolve around us, and that other people have needs equal to if not on many occasions superior to our own. Churchill, it seems, never grew up in this way, and remained entirely self-centred all his life. This again explains his entirely egocentric behaviour towards others.

However, the compensatory 'phantasy' to which Storr refers shows that we owe our survival in 1940 to Churchill's warped inner self. Such depressives, it appears, have fantasy feelings about being heroes – something Churchill, not a natural strongman, evidenced in his feats of danger and adventure even as a young soldier – and Churchill also had the feeling that Providence or Destiny (he was never particularly religious) preserved him for a great task in which he would ride to the rescue and save the equivalent of the damsel in distress. In Britain, in 1940, precisely such a moment arose, and it should be said that while today Britons cheer Churchill to the rafters for saving the West from fascism, it is also true to say, as we saw in the first chapter, that the odds against Britain surviving Nazi Germany in 1940 were so monumental that most normal people would have given up in despair, precisely as the French did to Hitler in June 1940. Churchill, however, felt certain that he could save Britain from conquest as no one else could, and thank goodness that he did.

Churchill's wartime physician Lord Moran was well aware of his patient's unusual psychological make-up, as Storr comments in quoting him:

> One of the most remarkable features of Churchill's psychology is that this conviction persisted throughout the greater part of his life, until, at the age of sixty-five [in 1940] his phantasy found expression in reality. As he said to Moran, 'This cannot be an accident, it must be by design. I was kept for this job.' If Churchill had died in 1939 he would have been regarded as a failure. Moran is undoubtedly right when he writes that it was in the 'inner world of make-believe in which Winston found reality'. It is probable that England owed her survival in 1940 to this inner world of make-believe.

This assertion of depression also ties in, I think, with another comment that many have made on Churchill, including Hitler, namely that he was someone strongly dependent on a vast intake of alcohol all his adult life, even if he was not an actual alcoholic.

Alcoholism is often rightly described as masked depression, and alcohol dependency and depression often run in families. As we know from his physician Lord Moran's account, Churchill was a lifelong clinical depressive, with his 'Black Dog' moods. If one links, as it is medically correct to do, alcoholism and alcohol dependency with depression, there is therefore little doubt that Churchill's gargantuan alcohol intake is closely linked to his clinical depressive tendencies.

It thus makes possible sense that Churchill's frequently exhibited lack of feeling was a symptom of mental affliction, since sufferers from some conditions can show a lack of awareness of their impact on other people, and this was compounded by Churchill's egotism from infancy. While his contemporaries would also rightly have felt neglected by their parents, but have learned to cope with it, however reluctantly, for Churchill the damage remained and was an obsession, one upon which he never gave up, and which accounts for the nature of the sad letters home found in his book *My Early Life*.

Here it is worth saying that in writing about Churchill's 'Black Dog', Anthony Storr makes the point that creativity and depression also often go together. Churchill was certainly one of the most creative politicians of his age, as is shown by his fascination with technical innovation throughout his adult life; so it is possible that his depression actually helped. This is conjecture, of course, but it is an interesting hypothesis all the same.

A second thing both the traditional life story and more recent authors' accounts highlight is the hideous psychological impact that Lord Randolph Churchill's early death, when his son was barely out of adolescence, had upon him. Those who have seen the film *Young Winston* will know the popular legend, namely that his father, Lord Randolph Churchill, died while still only in his forties from what is euphemistically called General Paralysis of the Insane, the extreme mental disorder associated with tertiary syphilis, a disease, then as now, transmitted through sexual activity.

Today, experts such as the American physician John Mather argue that this diagnosis is, medically, entirely wrong. Neither Winston nor his brother Jack seem to have been affected in any way – as the movie concedes; and nor was Jenny Churchill either, and since the Churchill marriage was a rare love match, this in itself tells us something, as the other members of the family would have been infected with syphilis. The likelihood now is that Lord Randolph had some kind of brain tumour, which was more difficult to diagnose then than it would be today. This means that Lord Randolph's premature death was a tragedy, but not one with any implications of sexual misconduct and extra-marital shenanigans or moral taint.

But, and this is the key point, *the young Winston did not know that* and thus had the sense of shame and horror that one would expect from a son who really did believe that his father died of syphilis. Much of his early adult life was an attempt, in the form of biography, to prove that his father was a great man, and the notion that he was doing all possible to rehabilitate a parent whose disgrace was, in many ways, all too public, morally as well as politically, does make a great deal of sense.

Historians have also pointed out that Churchill was in many ways under-sexed, or, as it might be better to say, certainly not as over-sexed and promiscuous as many a Type A politician, from David Lloyd George, the British Prime Minister, to President J.F. Kennedy and countless others one can think of besides. It is possible that his revulsion at what he thought was his father's misbehaviour is linked to this, along with the fact that he was in his mid-thirties before getting married. (The fact, though, that his mother had a very active love life after his father's death, and that one of her subsequent husbands was younger than her own son, is, possibly just as psychologically significant, though this can only be speculation, since we have nothing from Churchill himself on this.)

Churchill's self-centredness probably put off those whom he was courting as a young man – his late marriage was not for want of proposing to several young women, Pamela Plowden being one, before Clementine Hozier finally accepted him. They had met, with no spark between them in 1904, but when they met again at a dinner party in 1908, romance blossomed. The granddaughter, through her mother, of an earl, but the daughter (legally at least) of an ordinary stockbroker, Clementine had had to make much of her own way in the world, and was to give her husband the ballast his life had always needed. As emerges from the correspondence during the rest of his life, Churchill was lyrically happy in his marriage, and devoted to Clementine right to the end. Perhaps it was that genuine uxorious joy that led him, unlike so many top politicians before or since, to stay faithful to one woman and to be an example for the virtues of monogamy. Here again his resolution deserves full praise.

Churchill's career in the military, upon which he embarked at the age of eighteen when he went to Sandhurst, is one about which we know much, not least because he wrote about it himself. He was in a cavalry hussar regiment, joining the 4th Hussars in February 1895, a socially elite group that caused his poor mother much financial hardship, as the lifestyle expected of an officer in one of the smarter regiments was far greater than her limited income could sustain. But unlike most of his contemporaries, the sheer boredom of regimental life, in his case in the British Raj in India, proved too much.

He was something of a bully towards those he regarded as weaklings. While bullying is an unpleasant trait in anyone, Churchill's antics were typical of the young officer class throughout the ages: certainly the dreadful initiation rites at many a military academy in Britain or the United States until very recent times shows us that his mean behaviour was by no means exceptional, not that this is an excuse those of us whose lives have been exclusively civilian would accept today.

Churchill, as many of his biographers have been so right to suggest, was a man steeped in Empire. He was an imperialist to the last bone in his body, and the young subaltern of the British Raj in the late 1890s was to inform the great national leader he was to be during the Second World War, and indeed throughout his political career of over six decades. As we will see much later on, however, when we contemplate his zealous refusal to allow India its long overdue independence, this was frequently to be a *disadvantage* rather than a bonus. But one can also argue that there was, especially in 1940–1, a silver lining, in that it gave him a lifelong patriotism and sense of British destiny that was to stand him and his besieged nation in good stead when Hitler was but a short distance across the English Channel.

So we can look at this either way: a bad characteristic when it came to suppressing the desire for freedom for hundreds of millions of Indians (and other colonial subjects), but an asset when it came to the crisis of 1940 and the oratory he was able to employ in favour of Britain and the values of Western civilization against Nazi barbarity.

Churchill was a relentless self-promoter all his life. Many a young officer had exciting adventures on the legendary North West Frontier (much of which is now in Pakistan), fighting wars against recalcitrant natives, playing polo – Churchill was particularly good at this game – and other manly feats of similar nature. But only Churchill turned them into bestselling books that made him famous while still in his early twenties.

In 1896, aged just twenty-one, Churchill was posted with his regiment to Bangalore, now famous as the capital of Indian outsourcing and high technology, but then a more traditional town in the British Raj. Inactivity did not suit Churchill, and he soon found the opportunity to win his spurs in battle against the enemies of the Empire, in actions reminiscent of scenes familiar to readers of Rudyard Kipling and to countless generations of Victorian boys who loved tales of dash and daring. He was allocated to the Malakand Field Force of the suitably named General Sir Bindon Blood. By 1897 he was with the Force attacking rebellious Pathan tribes (now familiar to us as the Pashtun, the tribal grouping powerful in both Pakistan and Afghanistan, whom British and American forces were to be found fighting in the early years of the twenty-first century).

Fortunately for posterity, Churchill survived. Not only did he send copious journalistic pieces to various influential newspapers – something no young officer would be allowed to do today – but he also turned an account of his experiences into his first bestseller, the eponymous *The Malakand Field Force.* Not long after this he was near Peshawar, fighting yet more tribesmen, the Afridis, in the Raj's Tirah Campaign.

Most soldiers stay with their regiments for decades, until death or retirement. Such rules did not apply to Churchill however. He was an unashamed string-puller, using shamelessly his mother's contacts and social popularity to make sure that he was wherever the action might be.

So, while his regimental colleagues had to stay behind, Churchill was off, finding new wars and new conflicts, not just to fight in them but also with the long-term goal of keeping himself in the public eye, as a hero about whom all would soon be talking.

In October 1897 he made a private detour – to Cuba. He was not really there as a soldier, but as a self-appointed war correspondent, watching the soon to be vain Spanish attempt to crush the Cuban desire for independence. Churchill was not there for long, but it did help him to learn to write journalistic dispatches, something that was to stand him in good stead for most of his life, especially during his time in the political wilderness in the 1930s when journalism was to be the financial mainstay of his increasingly extravagant lifestyle.

And as Geoffrey Best reminds us, he also acquired a habit that would make him famous and give him one of his most loved wartime characteristics: the Havana Cigar. Often he would not smoke it down but wave it around, with sweeping gestures, as part of his air of resolute defiance against the enemy. He also, Best points out, picked up the Hispanic custom of the siesta, of sleeping if possible in the afternoon. While this is certainly the norm in hot climates, it is not so common in cooler climes such as Britain's, however, and for much of Churchill's life he was up against colleagues and subordinates who worked in the afternoon but wanted to go home at night, whereas Churchill, reinvigorated by his nap, would be wide awake and active until very late at night. This, his wartime military and political subordinates found, was a habit they wished he had not acquired . . .

Then in late 1898, his wanderlust, as before away from his regiment, took him thousands of miles to what is now the Sudan. But also, that same year his first and only novel, *Savrola*, a swashbuckling adventure tale, not unlike, perhaps, the *Sharpe* novels of Bernard Cornwell, was published. Churchill never had another go at fiction – it was not really his forte – but at the time the book was highly useful in keeping his profile permanently in the public gaze back home.

The Sudan – now the biggest country geographically in Africa, and one with a long history of civil war – was theoretically under the rule of the Egyptian Khedive, who in theory was a subject of the Ottoman Empire but who in practice, since 1882, had been under British control. The British had tried in the 1880s to bring this whole area under their command, but in 1884 a local Islamic leader and mystic, the Mahdi, had risen in revolt, and, with the imperial rescue force unable to get to the capital, Khartoum, the British force there under General Gordon was massacred. Gordon, who had earlier served in wars in China, was a popular hero, and his death caused serious political damage to the Gladstone government back home. By 1898 the British had the will and the means to reclaim lost territory, and a major expeditionary force was sent out under Field Marshal Kitchener, himself like Gordon a popular general back in the United Kingdom.

Churchill, through his mother's connections, tried to obtain a post on Kitchener's staff. But Kitchener, the sirdar, or commander, of the notionally Egyptian Army, was a homosexual oblivious to the charms of Churchill's mother. But Jenny was able to pull other strings on her son's behalf, and soon the young Winston found himself with a commission in another cavalry regiment on the one hand, and with a writing commission from the influential Conservative newspaper the *Morning Post*, on the other. He was now all set for another war.

The Battle of Omdurman, in which modern British soldiers beat an army of vastly inferior technology, has been called the last great cavalry charge of the British Army. Strictly speaking this is untrue, as many Australian and British cavalry regiments fought in the Middle East against the Ottoman forces in the First World War.

But the romance of Omdurman remains, and, needless to say, Churchill was there, in the thick of the battle, on horseback and on several occasions during the fighting close to death. It also goes without saying that he loved every minute of it, and wrote it all up, first for the newspapers and then in a two-volume work, of nearly a thousand pages in total, called *The River War*.

Once again he was famous, and so he now decided that the time had come for his first foray into politics. He had to resign his commission to do this, so he returned to Bangalore, where he was able to play a lot more polo before coming back to England and attempting to win a seat. His first try was in the Lancashire textile town of Oldham, in the north-west. He had no links with this area, and it was a failure.

Beaten though he may have been, he determined that he would continue to be a man of action. Now, in 1899, that meant South Africa, where the war between the British Empire and the Dutch Boers, inhabitants of two white settler republics, were at war. He swiftly gained a journalist contract, and, whether by luck or design, found himself on the same ship out to Africa as the Commander-in-Chief, Sir Redvers Buller.

Sometimes bad fortune can turn good, and this was now the case with the daring young ace correspondent for the *Morning Post* when he was captured by the Boers. Churchill claimed that he was a mere journalist, but his pleas of civilian status did not impress his Boer captors. (Having foolishly left his Mauser on the train that he was defending, he had jettisoned the bullets in his pockets in the nick of time. This might have been just as well for posterity, though, as he might otherwise have been shot.)

Also taken into captivity was a friend from India days, a regular officer called Aylmer Haldane. People back home lobbied for a reward for bravery for him, but his civilian status ruled that out – he never gained a gallantry medal during his entire military career, and it is ironic that the episode in which he probably acted more courageously than any other failed to earn him one because his official non-combatant status made it impossible.

Churchill's capture gained him huge publicity, which he was able, characteristically, to turn swiftly to his advantage. After a short time in prison, in a converted school in one of the Boer capitals, Pretoria, he and Haldane and another officer plotted an escape. All of them were supposed to get out of prison camp together, but in the end only Churchill made it out, leaving the others behind. This was great news for him, but later came to haunt him, since Haldane was not at all happy at being left behind and still a prisoner. But after a long and very exciting journey, recounted later with enormous verve in the book he wrote about it, he managed finally, with many adventures, to make it to freedom in Portuguese-ruled territory, now Mozambique. He was then able to take a ship to Durban, where he decided to join the Territorial Army, the South African Light Horse.

He was not a proper soldier and his salary as a journalist was twelve times that of his notional military rank. Technically speaking, combining journalism and a commission was not allowed – the War Office had tightened up the regulations – but as always Churchill was permitted to bend the rules. He fought in several engagements against the Boers, at a major defeat for the British at Spion Kop and then at one of the last great military victories of the Victorian era at the relief of the siege of Ladysmith, a turning of the tide for the British who had hitherto been doing really badly against their less well armed but far craftier Boer opponents. At a minor skirmish at a place called Dewetsdorp his horse was killed from underneath him, and he was fortunate to escape unscathed.

By 1900 the war had two years still to run, and all regular soldiers had to remain until British victory in 1902. Churchill, by contrast, had returned home, to fight Oldham again as a Conservative, in the 'Khaki Election' that the Government held that year to garner maximum votes from the turn in Britain's favour in the conflict. This time he was successful and became a Member of Parliament at last. His military career was over, its purpose successful. Needless to say, he was able to write another book about his adventures, *London to Ladysmith via Pretoria*, and this too was a financially successful bestseller.

His career seemed made. All that had eluded him was marriage – his attempt to woo Pamela Plowden in 1899 had failed, and most biographers agree that as a young man Churchill was too obsessed with politics, too self-centred or egotistical to impress the opposite sex. But in all other respects things were going according to plan: in 1900 Winston Churchill was the coming man.

As one of his many biographers John Keegan states, 'Yet though politics was to consume Churchill's later youth, adulthood and maturity, his military years must be counted among the most significant of his life.' For not only did Churchill retain, as we saw earlier, the views of Empire of a subaltern on the North West Frontier, war was part of his persona, the love of action, the preference for boldness, dash and daring. So while he now became a civilian, he was, in a real sense, always a former soldier, a veteran, who saw things another way.

3

THE RISING STAR

In 1900 Churchill was elected a Conservative MP, as part of that party's memorable landslide success. He was to retire from the House of Commons in 1964, a unique length of service in the House of Commons, interrupted only briefly when having to stand for re-election before the First World War under arcane rules for office-holders, and again in the 1920s when he switched sides and was briefly without a seat. This longevity is part of what makes him special, and throughout his parliamentary career he was to hold his membership of the House and his responsibility to it as a minister in later years with the utmost reverence. To him, the Commons represented all that was best about Britain, its Empire and how it ran its business. Even as Prime Minister during the Second World War he never omitted to explain as much to the House of Commons as possible, the need for confidentiality notwithstanding. All this was ahead of him though, and when he joined as a very junior MP he did not allow himself to sit comfortably.

But as always with Churchill it was not that simple . . . In 1904 he was to defect to the Opposition and become a Liberal MP, remaining as one until 1922. He was then to stand as a Constitutionalist, finally becoming a Conservative MP again in 1924. He entered politics as a hero, but was soon to get a less pleasing epithet: maverick. Even upon election, Churchill was not always with his party, even on the great issue of the day, the Boer War. (The Liberal opposition on this was split, between those who were pro-Boer and those who supported the expansion of the British Empire.)

Despite his warrior experience, Churchill first made his name in politics attacking the Secretary of State for War, St John Brodrick, especially the latter's wish to expand the Army to at least three full corps. Churchill argued that, by contrast, Britain's glory was the Royal Navy, and the command of the seas. Having three corps would be too many to fight 'savages' and not enough to oppose the mighty armies on the continent, which had as many as twenty army corps each. In terms of where Britain saw itself at that time, he was surely right. While it was true that the Boer War showed up many of the inadequacies of the British Army, nevertheless the United Kingdom's role was principally naval, to defend the trade routes, and the Army's to serve both at home and also when needed in the Empire, most notably in India, where Churchill had recently served.

Yet Churchill was also profoundly mistaken, as things turned out for Britain during the twentieth century. For it is possible to argue that because Britain would soon be fighting a war on the continent of Europe – as it would again during the Second World War – what was *really* needed was in fact an even bigger Army than Brodrick himself was proposing: three Army corps were not too many, as Churchill was stating, but in fact far too few. The wars of the twentieth century were not primarily to be against 'savages' in Africa or on the North West Frontier of India, but in Europe, against countries with massive land armies, such as Germany. But it is also fair to say that Churchill was by no means alone in failing to see this, and indeed the lack of a major continental fighting army was to be a major problem during the next forty years.

On the other hand, historians have pointed out three plusses in Churchill's attacks. Churchill understood the nature of modern war in that he foresaw accurately the devastating effect that recent weapons technology could unleash: a prediction that would be fulfilled in the carnage of the trenches after 1914. He also understood the need for national prosperity in order to maintain an army and, thirdly, he emphasized what he believed to be the moral superiority of Britain and its democratic way of life. In attacking his *own* government Winston was following in the footsteps of his father, Randolph, who had done exactly the same thing decades earlier. Indeed, there was almost an excess of filial piety on the son's part, as Churchill now seemed to make himself as much like his father as possible. He joined a group of bumptious young Conservative politicians nicknamed the 'Hughligans' after their leader, Lord Hugh Cecil, and he was far from liked on his own side, let alone by the Opposition.

His first years at Westminster also saw the beginning of the famous Churchill rhetoric. This did not come naturally to him – an important difference between rhetoric and oratory – but through enormous pains whenever he made a speech. He would write and rewrite a speech many times, as one can see when looking at the original notes – and he would then learn it by heart. In later years this would give us the great wartime speeches with which we are so familiar, and which completely transformed the morale of the British people in 1940–1. But when he commenced his career, such facility was if anything a disadvantage. Rhetoric from a young man could seem overblown; it also meant that he did not think quickly on his feet, since all his speeches were prepared sometimes days beforehand, and this did not give him the flexibility that orators, such as the up and coming Welsh politician David Lloyd George, possess with ease. Oratory can be spontaneous, but rhetoric, while stirring, seems to find that more difficult, and Churchill's powerful rhetorical gift was, at this stage in his life, a mixed blessing.

Soon the son found himself in a very different place from his father, as the issue of free trade came to split the Conservative Party. In 1903 the Cabinet came asunder, with the great protectionist politician Joseph Chamberlain quitting the government because he favoured that policy over free trade, and with others resigning, because the Government was not for free trade enough, with Churchill quitting the party the following year.

Chamberlain wanted to protect Britain's international industrial position by introducing tariff barriers against foreign trade – Germany and the United States were now growing greatly in terms of innovation and exports – and impose 'imperial preference', which would have meant allowing tax-free imports from Canada and Australia, for example, while imposing taxes on those from, say, Germany or France, even though the latter two countries were closer geographically. Churchill would have none of this, supporting instead the principle of universal free trade without fiscal barriers, something believed in equally strongly by the Liberal Party of the time and also many across the Atlantic in the United States.

Then, in 1904, Churchill switched sides and became a Liberal. In politics those who change political allegiance are regarded with grave suspicion, and this switch was to mark Churchill for many years to come. In particular, the Conservatives found it hard to trust him again, and his move only confirmed his maverick status in the eyes of many of the more staid members of that party, a reputation that was to dog him even after he rejoined the Conservatives in 1924, right down to his becoming their leader in 1940 and, for some, even beyond. 'Crossing the floor', as it is known in Britain, is still comparatively rare, and whoever does so forever forfeits the right of being called 'a sound party man (or woman)'. Churchill was, of course, very much his own man, which did not help his reputation among the dullards who always toed the line.

Would it have made any difference, as some have suggested, if the Conservative Prime Minister, the languid philosopher-politician Arthur Balfour, had given Churchill a position in the Government? It is hard to know, and while not all agreed, then as now, whether Churchill was sincere in his conversion to free trade, there is no reason why his stance should be considered other than genuine. In any case, the ferocity of his attacks on Brodrick made it highly unlikely that he would ever have achieved office in a Balfour administration.

By 1905 the Conservative Government, despite having a large parliamentary majority, simply could not hold itself together any more, and so resigned, even before a general election was called (which came in 1906). Churchill now became Parliamentary Under-Secretary of State for the Colonies, achieving office at last, and in a *Liberal* Government. Not only that, but since his Secretary of State, the Earl of Elgin, was in the House of Lords, Churchill was the representative of this important department in the House of Commons. He had finally arrived in power.

His career as a minister got off to a shaky start. His speeches, being filled with rhetoric, were far too overblown for most mundane matters, and, as noted, his reliance on prepared speeches made it hard for him to change tack in response to the cut and thrust of parliamentary debate. Having laid into Brodrick just a few years before, he was now on the defence himself, a minister facing criticism rather than a backbencher doling it out.

Not much has been written about Churchill's time as a junior minister in 1905–8, but it was a vital apprenticeship for future and higher office – and good training for when he became Secretary of State for the Colonies in 1921–2. As someone who had crossed the floor, he had had to find a new seat in Parliament, and in the Liberal landslide of 1906 had became MP for Manchester North

West, not too far away from his original Oldham constituency. There was a large Jewish minority in the area, and he was soon taking up the concerns of Jewish constituents. While many of his social class were anti-Semitic, Churchill never was; in fact, he was probably the most pro-Jewish, if not actually pro-Zionist, of all Britain's great twentieth-century politicians.

In 1908, while still only thirty-three, Churchill came into the Cabinet, the ministerial elite, as President of the Board of Trade. This was as part of the new Asquith administration, and, under the rules that then existed Churchill had to resign his seat and fight a by-election on appointment to the Cabinet. Unfortunately he lost, and it was lucky for him that a seat in the Scottish jute town of Dundee fell fortuitously vacant. This was to be his perch in Parliament until 1922. He had no links with Scotland, but in those days such things did not matter, and he was to prove a faithful MP for his Scottish constituents during his fourteen years with them.

That year also saw the most wonderful thing that ever happened to him, without which much of the rest of his life might not have been possible: his marriage to Clementine Hozier.

As we saw, his rather monomaniac personality put women off him. Thankfully, with Clementine, this did not happen. She was from an unhappy home, her legal father being Colonel Sir Henry Hozier, who left her mother, Lady Blanche Hozier, daughter of the Scottish aristocrat the Earl of Airlie, when she was young. (It is not known for sure who Clementine's biological father was – there are, as always, several theories: she was what

Arthur Balfour once described as one of the 'children of the mist'.) So although she was highly born, she was not at all wealthy, and had been obliged to make her way for herself, as would not have been the case with most aristocratic women of her time.

Striking-looking but not beautiful, Clementine was above all highly intelligent, and this seems to have been something Churchill, to his great credit, valued far above mere fleeting beauty. When they married in September 1908 – he having proposed to her in the park at Blenheim the previous month – it was to be both a true partnership that was rare among upper-class marriages of that time and a genuine love match.

Churchill remained utterly devoted to Clementine the rest of his life, during their entire and sometimes stormy fifty-seven years together. On his side, he was lyrically happy, and one of the most moving things one can do is to read their five decades of correspondence together, now collected and in print. She cannot have found someone as self-centred and histrionic as her husband easy to live with, but she stayed with him through thick and thin. Apart from a brief affair on a foreign holiday that she *might* have had in the 1930s, she was as totally faithful to him as he was to her, and in an age where many upper-class marriages were a sham, and in which divorce was slowly becoming allowed even in their circles, this too was a major blessing and achievement for them both.

Above all, as well as giving him the solid bedrock of a happy marriage, she kept her feet firmly on the ground, especially when, later on, his spending and lifestyle were to prove well beyond his financial means. She was also probably a liberal, if not Liberal, all her life, including when he was once again a Conservative MP.

In 1908, Churchill had replaced David Lloyd George at the Board of Trade, a job that then also included labour relations as well as responsibility for exports and industry. Lloyd George could not have come from a more different background – he had been a small town solicitor in north Wales, from a background utterly lacking in privilege or social connection. He was the radical firebrand par excellence of Welsh Liberalism, and in 1908 had been promoted to the second most powerful post in the Cabinet, Chancellor of the Exchequer, in charge of the nation's finances. For someone with his political radicalism and lack of wealth this was an amazing achievement. He seized the opportunity with both hands, and in 1909 put forward the most progressive, radical budget in British history. He was, in effect, introducing the Welfare State to Britain, something we now take for granted, but which, in Edwardian Britain, was seen by some almost as revolutionary.

However, the House of Lords then did something unprecedented: they rejected the budget. This created a terrible constitutional crisis, resolved only by two general elections in 1910, both of which were won by the Liberals, but with drastically reduced majorities, and dependent on Irish votes. During these debates, Churchill roundly attacked the House of Lords, which meant lambasting his own cousin, the Duke of Marlborough, and the aristocratic background from which both of them came. While Churchill's speeches were thoroughly defensible, they did not endear him to the party he had renounced in 1904.

The period of 1908–11 was Churchill's radical phase. The claims of his son Randolph, in the official biography, that his father helped to create the Welfare State, as President of the Board of Trade 1908–10, and then Home Secretary 1910–11, are probably exaggerated, as the full credit should go to Lloyd George. But there is no doubt that Churchill did a great deal to improve the lot of the ordinary working man, through the Acts of Parliament passed, for example, on insurance for those who had lost their jobs and on the conditions in which miners worked, legislation that he either steered through or helped to initiate. He was by this time a loyal follower of Lloyd George, and the combination of poorly born Welshman and English aristocrat was a potent one, with Lloyd George very much in the lead.

His time as Home Secretary, albeit a brief one, was not to help his future prospects, however. His problem was to be the law and order aspects of the post. One of many issues he faced was that of the suffragettes, the campaigners for votes for women. Churchill himself favoured giving women the vote – he was happily married to one of the most intelligent women of the day – but the problem was that the suffragettes regularly broke the law in order to make their voice heard. Sometimes they would be arrested, go on hunger strike and then have to be force-fed to prevent them from dying. This treatment created a huge row, and Churchill, while wishing that the women would employ different tactics, helped them by giving those arrested political prisoner status in gaol.

But it was labour unrest that caused the real difficulties for him, and was to blot his escutcheon for many years to come with the trade union movement.

By far the biggest and most aggravated dispute was in the Welsh town of Tonypandy, in the Rhondda valley, the heartland of the South Wales mining community, and of the newcomer to the political scene, the then still-infant Labour Party. There had already been riots, with broken windows and similar incidents, but what made an already febrile situation far worse was the decision by Churchill to send in troops as well as police, in this case a detachment of Lancashire Fusiliers. Order was eventually restored, but not until a great deal of bad feeling had been created, with Ramsay MacDonald, the eminent Labour politician, accusing the Government of making Wales like imperial Germany, since using the Army in place of the civil power was something that had not happened in Britain for decades and was highly unusual.

Churchill's defenders point out that he had been highly restrained elsewhere, notably in some quite acrimonious railway disputes, and that his decision to send troops to Tonypandy was a reluctant one. While that might have been true in Wales, however, he was also to send them in again, to solve the docks strike in London, while more moderate and conciliatory members of the Government, including his mentor David Lloyd George, preferred ordinary negotiation in a much less heated atmosphere.

As always, there are arguments on both sides. Churchill in his speeches always insisted upon the difference between Liberalism – in which he believed strongly – and socialism, which he rejected. This speech he made in 1908 shows clearly where he was coming from:

> Socialism seeks to pull down wealth; liberalism seeks to raise up poverty. Socialism would destroy private interests, Liberalism would preserve [them] . . . by reconciling them with public right. Socialism would kill enterprise; Liberalism would rescue enterprise from the trammels of privilege and preference. Socialism assails the preeminence of the individual; Liberalism seeks . . . to build up a minimum standard for the mass. Socialism exalts the rule; Liberalism exalts the man. Socialism attacks capitalism; Liberalism attacks monopoly.

The philosophical differences between the gradualism of the Liberal Party and the wish of the then socialist Labour Party to change society can here be seen. Churchill's two books of speeches at this time, *Liberalism and the Social Problem* and *The People's Rights*, show the direction in which his mind was going. But it is true to say that what Liberalism was trying to do was to ameliorate social problems, while the Labour Party sought to change the system itself. Ordinary people were greatly helped by Churchill's welfare reforms, but the class structure of which he was a part was not changed. However, it is worth pointing out that Britain did not suffer the level of violence from strikes and lock-outs that occurred in countries from France to the United States, and both the moderation of the British Trade Union leadership and the wisdom of Liberal politicians such as Churchill played a role in this. Indeed, the threat to law and order was to come not from the left, but from Churchill's former Conservative colleagues, and over Irish home rule, rather than revolution.

One can see in Churchill the benevolent aristocrat, being nice to the poor, and wanting genuinely to help them, but still believing in the *noblesse oblige* of his social class. But calling in the troops does question his judgement, and was a political mistake that played into the hands of extremists who wanted to foment revolution, as opposed to the mainstream trade unionists, who wanted rights for the workers but not the violent overthrow of the state along with them.

The other misjudgement Churchill made at this time was also a classic overreaction: the Siege of Sidney Street. Here again he brought in troops, and in this case also took a hand in directing events, being sure to be photographed by the press in the process. An anarchist nicknamed 'Peter the Painter' and a bunch of fellow Latvian desperadoes had holed themselves up in Sidney Street, in the East End of London. They had just killed three policemen, so feelings locally were running high, but whether Scots Guards were necessary to deal with them, and whether Churchill needed to be there in person are both moot points. Two bodies were found in the house, but 'Peter the Painter' seemed to have slipped away.

Both these incidents show a strong melodramatic streak in Churchill's personality, and each gave him a reputation, however unfair, for not being entirely balanced, and for being a self-seeking publicist, since his physical presence to direct operations was thought unnecessary.

None of this hindered his political career at the time, however. In 1911 he was granted the job in Government for which he is most famous. That year the Royal Navy was still the greatest fleet in the world, bigger still than the German imperial fleet that had been doing so much to catch up with its British rival. With international relations worsening rather than improving, the Admiralty urgently needed a First Lord who would be sure to get the Navy ready for anything that might happen. The Army was finally being modernized, and no one was better equipped to do the same for the fleet than Winston Churchill.

One of the main characteristics that Churchill possessed throughout his career was that of complete and utter dedication and enthusiasm for whatever he was asked to do. His time at the Admiralty was no exception. As Churchill wrote in one of his many autobiographies, his appointment was 'the biggest thing that has ever come my way – the chance I should have chosen before all others.'

As the famous rhyme goes:

> Rule Britannia!
> Britannia rule the waves
> Britons never, never, never shall be slaves . . .

There is no doubt that at the heart of Britain's sense of self-esteem was not just the vast extent of the British Empire, but also the Royal Navy, whose effortless command of the seas made so much of that dominion possible.

We need to put Churchill's role in this into context first. Parties of the politically progressive side of politics do not normally engage in massive military expansion. But the Liberal Governments of 1905–14 were the exception, especially with their vital and sorely needed reforms of the Army by Robert Haldane, Secretary of State for War – someone who, ironically, in the light of his building up of the British Army to fight Germany, had to leave office because he was hounded when war began for having studied in Germany and for having personal ties to many German intellectuals, whose horror at Prussian militarism probably reflected his own.

Haldane not only got the British Army into fighting condition, but made one other very important change: the introduction of a proper Imperial General Staff, one that was able to match the legendary German/Prussian equivalent that had proved so deeply effective in beating France and whose plans to fight modern warfare were both professional and highly skilled. Britain could not fight a twentieth-century war with eighteenth-century staff and planning methods, and Haldane was successful in ensuring that the Army was duly brought up to speed.

This was not however the case with the Royal Navy, and though Churchill eventually succeeded in getting a Naval Staff, this was only in the teeth of opposition from the naval members of the Admiralty.

In battleships, Germany was also the main threat, but in Churchill's time, Britain was ahead with the new, state-of-the-art Dreadnought class of battleship. This ship made all others obsolete, and gave supremacy to whoever had the most. The Dreadnought was a British invention, and therefore the Royal Navy was able to be the first off the starting block in twentieth-century naval technology.

The problem was that the German Navy was of particular interest to the Kaiser and was able, through its senior command, particularly Admiral Tirpitz, to spend as much money as was needed with the specific task of catching up with its British rivals. So it began building its own versions of the Dreadnought, and a deadly arms race now began. This entailed vast expenditure by the British, in order simply to stay ahead of the Germans fast enough to maintain the kind of naval supremacy and cutting edge that the Royal Navy regarded as its birthright. The sums involved were huge, however, and the Liberals as a party were as keen to improve the lot of the poor as they were to increase defence spending on enormous new battleships. Not only that, but as one historian has put it, 'although the navy's shipbuilding programme went far towards checking . . . [its] quantitive and qualitative decline, its ethos remained distinctly pre-modern'.

It was this challenge that the Prime Minister, Herbert Asquith, sent Churchill to the Admiralty in order to overcome. Therefore Churchill, who had opposed increasing naval spending in 1909, during his radical phase, when he was President of the Board of Trade, now became its leading advocate. Yet, as Richard Holmes has observed with regret about Churchill's tenure, 'The unasked question is whether or not Winston changed the culture of the Royal Navy, and the simple answer is that he fell far short.'

To his credit, though, Churchill was the politician who realized the importance of oil as it, instead of coal, was by far the best way to power ships on the high seas. His decision for the Government to purchase a major share in the Anglo-Persian Oil Company (now BP), one of the biggest oil companies in the world, shows how Churchill understood the needs of modern technology; and, perhaps uniquely among the political classes, he was happy to give scientists, the 'boffins', the support they needed to invent new ways of fighting war – a trait that was to remain a hallmark throughout his political career.

Similarly, though we primarily think of the tank, that essential component of modern war, as an army machine, it was in fact invented partly thanks to Churchill, having its origins during his tenure of the Admiralty, when he called it a 'land ship' and then coming to fruition when he was the Minister of Munitions towards the end of the First World War. Even the famous 'Mulberry Harbours' that enabled the landing of a vast army on the beaches of Normandy in 1944 have as their genesis a classic Churchillian brainwave from the First World War. He also invented the Royal Naval Air Service, and this was to transform warfare, since the Army then invented the Royal Flying Corps, which, when Churchill was Secretary of State for Air after 1919, became a wholly new and independent service, the Royal Air Force. So in these few years, he can claim to have changed the entire nature of fighting and with permanent results.

However, it was the culture of the Royal Navy that Churchill, despite his enthusiasm and instinctive support for technological change, was never effectively to change. And as far as upgrading the Navy's ships is concerned, here historians disagree with each other. Some think that he introduced the right types of battleships, while others feel that some of the classes of ship were not needed, especially for the kind of war that would exist when conflict broke out in 1914, while other needs were ill-supplied – in particular the British transport ships required to convoy supplies from the United States across the Atlantic. Either way, though, the Royal Navy was ready when war broke out in 1914, and while there were certainly reverses along the way, the Navy proved at least the equal of the German fleet, if never its superior, and of that Churchill can be proud.

4

THE FALLING STAR

In 1914 Britain found itself at war, not just with Germany and the Austro-Hungarian Empire, but after the Ottomans decided to join the German side, with that ancient empire, which ruled over much of today's Middle East and Turkey, as well.

At the time, the conflict – the biggest and most widespread since the Napoleonic Wars of a century earlier – was the bloodiest and most global in history, hence its name at the time, the Great War. Because of its international reach, we are now right to call it the First World War, since it encompassed not just war in Europe and in the Middle East, but also the colonial possessions of the European powers in Africa and Asia as well. This was war of a kind not seen before, and one in which the protagonists failed utterly to comprehend the new level of slaughter that modern technology would bring, a lesson they could have learned, but had not, from the carnage wrought with similar weaponry in the American Civil War.

So there was a Western Front with Germany, in Belgium and France – the part of the war where most of the British casualties occurred – and an Eastern Front, against the Ottoman Empire, centred mainly on what we now call the Middle East and also in the Balkans, where the conflict had begun in August 1914.

The main enemy, Germany, was on Britain's Western Front, and this is where most of the action took place during 1914–18, with colossal loss of life. But there was another strategy, namely that of hitting the enemy where it was deemed to be vulnerable, rather than at its strongest point. Churchill was a strong believer in victory this way, and he had the brainwave of deciding that one of the best ways to finish the war would be to open up a second front against Germany's militarily weaker allies, in this case the Ottoman Empire in particular, and also, perhaps, Bulgaria. This was known as the Easterner strategy, from the Ottoman Empire's geographical location, and it was followed against that empire in what is now Iraq, with what were soon to prove disastrous results, at a town called Kut.

Churchill noticed that the capital of the Ottoman Empire, Constantinople (now Istanbul) was vulnerable to a sea-borne attack, through the Dardanelles, the narrow straits that lead from the Mediterranean through to the Sea of Marmora, then to the Bosphorus (on either side of which Constantinople is situated) and thence to the Black Sea. This was a very risky plan, though, since it needed good luck, strong inter-service co-ordination and great speed, as the straits would need to be captured before the Ottoman army could send reinforcements. Unfortunately for Churchill, such a strategy was impossible, since his department, the Admiralty, had no power over the War Office, which controlled the Army. He could only command the Royal Navy, and hope that the Army would be able to follow through.

In essence, the Royal Navy would bombard the Ottoman fortifications on both sides of the Dardanelles, proceed through the Sea of Marmora, and then attack the capital, Constantinople, with the idea of putting the Ottoman Empire out of the war. This would remove one of Germany's allies, and it would also have the effect of easing pressure on the sclerotic and militarily hard-pressed Russian Empire, which was finding great difficulty fighting the Germans, the Austrians and the Ottomans simultaneously. Victory in the East would also improve the military stalemate in the West, especially on the Flanders front line, the trenches.

This was the peripheral approach that, as indicated earlier, Churchill would later adopt during the critical 1940–1 campaign of the Second World. Churchill thought his assault on Turkey would be a strike against the soft target of the Ottoman Empire rather than the harder one of imperial Germany. However, this is where things began increasingly to unravel . . .

The naval bombardment did not work. The Royal Navy lost ships, sunk by mines and by enemy fire, and thus did not even get near Constantinople. Furthermore, the naval battery lasted weeks, with not a single soldier landing, since the Secretary of State for War, the aged Field Marshal Lord Kitchener, decreed that there were not enough troops available for an immediate landing. In addition, the naval raid alerted the Turks to possible British action, completely destroying the element of surprise. So when the Army, under the command of the sadly highly deficient General Sir Ian Hamilton, an old friend of Churchill's from the latter's military days, began the assault on the Gallipoli peninsula in April 1915, the result was destined to be carnage before even the first troops had landed.

One thing should be said. In Australia and in New Zealand, the Dardanelles campaign is remembered with especial sorrow and anti-British venom, with understandable reason, because of the particularly high casualties sustained by the Australian and New Zealand Army Corps (ANZAC) troops. The sufferings of the Antipodean soldiers was very real and truly terrible, but then so were those of the British soldiers obliged to fight there too.

Breakthrough by the Allies proved to be completely impossible, thanks to the resistance of the Turks, whose defences were greatly helped by the ability of their Turkish commander (there were German officers there too) Mustafa Kemal, soon to be famous, after 1922, as Atatürk, the founder of present-day Turkey. Thus, outfought and out-generaled, the Western forces were obliged to make an ignominious retreat, with thousands having died entirely in vain. The results of fighting the Ottomans were the same in Mesopotamia (present-day Iraq), with thousands of British and Indian soldiers captured at Kut, the longest siege in the history of the British Army. The Turks had proved that they were not the soft target for which the British took them, and it was to take until 1917 for an Allied breakthrough, with the Australian cavalry regiments proving as magnificently victorious in Palestine as their infantry equivalents had been so terribly routed in defeat in Gallipoli.

When the redoubtable First Sea Lord Jacky Fisher fell out with Churchill over this debacle, and ran to the Leader of the Opposition, Bonar Law, he provoked a major political crisis. Churchill was forced to resign as First Lord of the Admiralty in May 1915, Fisher having quit himself just a short time before as First Sea Lord. In order to stay in power, the increasingly unsteady and often drunken Prime Minister, Herbert Asquith, had felt obliged to form a coalition with the Conservatives, and one of their terms for joining was that Churchill be sacked from the Admiralty – they still hated him for his defection back in 1904 to the Liberals over free trade. One of the key appointments was that of the former Conservative leader and Prime Minister Arthur Balfour as the new First Lord of the Admiralty, a safe pair of hands.

Churchill was given a ministry without portfolio, that of Chancellor of the Duchy of Lancaster, a post existing from the Middle Ages that still allows a Prime Minister to give a colleague government office but without any specific departmental responsibilities. Even this post did not last long, however – when the full measure of official investigations into the Dardanelles fiasco revealed how much had gone wrong, Churchill had to quit the Government altogether, in total shame. He felt that his political career was over – and at the age of forty, his father's fate nearly thirty years earlier. Would it be a case of 'like father, like son'?

Given the Conservatives' animosity towards Churchill for joining the Liberals, he might well have lost his post at the Admiralty anyway in a Coalition government. But to lose his job and to be so heavily censured for such a visible failure was a double blow, and it is thus not surprising, perhaps, that he thought he might well be suffering the same political ignominy as his father. Looking back on Churchill as we now know him, this seems incredible: that Britain's greatest military-political hero should have led his country into an epic disaster, and have perhaps never held political office again, let alone be Prime Minister during the country's most dire peril in the Second World War. Churchill's response also has a touch of the histrionic. After Churchill's death in 1965, Clementine confided in the biographer Martin Gilbert that the catastrophe at the Dardanelles in 1915, that was temporarily to derail her husband's meteoric rise to the top, was 'something that haunted him for the rest of his life. He always believed in it. When he left the Admiralty he thought he was finished. I thought he would never get over the Dardanelles. I thought he would die of grief.'

Churchill was fortunate that the debacle in the Dardanelles did not, in fact, finish his political career for good: a foolish resignation had destroyed his father's equally meteoric rise to the top back in 1886, in that case permanently. The Dardanelles did also have a dividend. As we have seen, Churchill's problem was that he had no say over what the Army did, and it was above all their disaster on the ground that sealed the expedition's fate and thus ensured Churchill's short-term political demise. Once he became Prime Minister in 1940, he immediately invented the title of Minister of Defence (hitherto a very amorphous Minister *for the Co-ordination* of Defence), with himself as its first holder. He was then able to co-ordinate British strategy far more effectively than would have been the case if the three relevant ministries (Admiralty, War, Air) had continued as independent kingdoms refusing to link up their plans and campaigns.

As First Lord of the Admiralty Churchill bore no responsibility for the mess in the Dardanelles created by the Army, which was entirely beyond his control. Nor did the Secretary of State for War, Field Marshal Lord Kitchener of Khartoum, have to carry any responsibility for what went wrong (in his case, dying conveniently when his ship was torpedoed, his involvement in the Gallipoli fiasco is now mainly forgotten).

In fact, Gallipoli was no worse a disaster than the battle of Kut, which is forgotten today. Gallipoli remains famous because of the ANZAC loss of life, and because Churchill did so much to defend himself at the time, and later in print; his zealous self-defence made people feel at the time that he was over-egging the pudding, and *that* did him no good at all. Contemporary politicians joked that Churchill wrote six volumes about himself and called it a history of the world! One can agree with those who call *The World Crisis* (published from 1923) hard going, since it is nothing like as exciting or enjoyable a read as his subsequent, and far more famous, six-volume *The Second World War*, which millions have read and still do so today.

The Dardanelles episode also demonstrates Churchill at both his best and at his very worst. On the credit side, it shows he could think 'out of the box' as we would now say, and come up with creative ideas that would be of enormous help in winning. With his support of the nascent Royal Air Force, and his advocacy of what was soon to become the tank, two vital developments in the Allies' eventual victory over Germany in 1918, we can see his thinking as being invaluable. But at the same time, his Dardanelles brainwave shows how such thinking can not only go seriously astray, but also cost thousands of human lives, as proved to be the case with all those British and ANZAC servicemen who died for what was essentially a wild goose chase of uncertain success.

Lloyd George had become Minister of Munitions, a new post, in the Coalition Government, with the plan of making good the shortage of shells on the Western Front that constituted the other big scandal of 1915. He did this superbly well, and was, the following year, able to use his success to overthrow Asquith and become Prime Minister.

Having returned to the ignominy of the backbenches, Churchill would be haunted by his reputation for unreliability and for rashness, something that was to dog him for years to come. In 1916 he spent five months at the front, no longer a discredited politician but a soldier, in charge of a battalion of the Royal Scots Greys, a regiment with which he had enjoyed no previous connection. This is an extraordinary episode in his career, and is in many ways without parallel, since when it was over he went from being on the front line of war to being a politician again.

He had originally wanted to command an entire brigade, despite having no experience whatsoever at so high a military grade. He even bought a brigadier's outfit. But his connections as a former Cabinet minister meant that he was very hard indeed to place, because while no one doubted his bravery, being in charge of a major government department is a civilian occupation that bears no resemblance to commanding men in action on the battlefield, as the senior generals well knew. So while he spent a short time at military headquarters, they had to discuss among themselves where on earth to put him. So, instead of becoming a full brigade commander, he ended up on part of the front in Belgium, in a town properly called Ploegsteert, but widely known by the British soldiers who fought there as 'Plugstreet'.

As so often in his life, Churchill spent some of his time there playing to the gallery. He insisted on wearing a French military hat, the one in which he is most famously photographed. But, realizing that he held the lives of his men very much in his hands – a bad command could cause their deaths as well as his – he soon adapted, and was popular among officers and men alike. In fact, the only difference that his fame back home meant for his troops was that he was able to get Clemmie to send huge amounts of very rare or impossible to obtain foodstuffs for everyone, so that for the short period for which he was with them, they were probably some of the best-fed front line troops in the army!

While the fighting was not at its worst in the Ploegsteert area when Churchill was there, he came close to death on many occasions, and he was able to experience life under fire in a way that was the case with virtually no other politician of the time. He was also able to meet and work alongside people of a very different social class to his own, something that was something profoundly useful for somebody like him, as it was also to be for those very numerous officers from aristocratic or upper-middle-class homes who would never normally have spent so prolonged and intimate a period with those from social backgrounds so deeply diverse, in a Britain where the gulf between classes was far bigger than it is today.

Here one can also say that Churchill did not suffer from the 'survivor's guilt' which inflicted itself on so many of the social elite who did survive the carnage, Churchill's future colleague, and eventual successor as Prime Minister, Sir Anthony Eden, being among them.

By 1917 Churchill was back in Westminster, his brief military interlude over. He had seen for himself the slaughter of the trenches, and had rightly been appalled by it. His thoughts towards the senior generals were not at all favourable, and he realized that one of the major reasons for the scale of the carnage was the lack of decent technical equipment to fight the war against a far more technologically advanced German army.

By this time, Lloyd George felt that enough water had gone under the bridge for Churchill to be brought back into Government, and he duly appointed him Minister of Munitions. Churchill seized the opportunity for political resurrection given to him by the Prime Minister with all his characteristic eagerness. He was back at the heart of power at last.

One of the machines that transformed warfare was the tank. As we saw, Churchill was already aware of its possible advantage when he was at the Admiralty. Now, as Minister of Munitions, he did all he could to advance its cause, despite the staunch opposition of the generals, for whom such modern devices were mere toys that diverted from the glory of actual combat on the field.

The tank was alas almost too late to make a major difference on the Western Front, but this did not prevent Churchill and his Ministry trying to get it produced in sufficient numbers. He knew that modern advances saved lives, and while millions were to die in the Second World War, the level of British military deaths was considerably lower in that conflict than in the First World War. While there were some aspects of the new warfare that Churchill never fully grasped, he was miles ahead of any of his colleagues in understanding the difference technological change made to fighting, at least in principle if not always in precise detail. When one considers that he had no scientific background of any kind, his unique grasp is the more impressive.

Like many of the officers who did survive the trenches – as he had done – Churchill also saw that the strategic concepts of the generals were both woefully lacking and also oblivious to the level of deaths that were caused by sending men armed only with bayonets against heavily fortified defences. In 1919 he became Secretary of State for War and also for Air, in charge of the creation of the infant Royal Air Force, as a separate and independent branch of the armed services.

Britain may have won the war, but the British state was all but bankrupt, as Churchill was very aware. He also discovered in his new job that instead of being able to demobilize the victorious but exhausted army, he was now responsible for a vast new array of military obligations, from Ireland in the west through to Iraq in the east, all of which were well above the financial ability of the British taxpayer to finance.

It is simpler to look at the two key areas in which he was deeply involved – the Middle East and Ireland – separately, but as we do so we should remember that for him, both these and his wider responsibilities elsewhere were equally pressing, and demanding of his time and the increasingly depleted national budget.

The first of these areas was the Middle East, for large swathes of which, in Mesopotamia and Palestine, Britain now had direct responsibility. They also needed huge armies to keep them under control, something which came under Churchill's mandate as Secretary of State for War.

The European – effectively Franco-British – creation of the Middle East after the First World War is frequently deemed to lie with those two much maligned men, Sir Mark Sykes and his French counterpart, M. Picot, who, between them, are supposed to have carved up the Middle East between them, entirely to the detriment of the Arab population. While it was actually more complex than this, the net result was that Britain was faced with some awesome post-war responsibilities for which no finances any longer existed.

The Ottoman Empire had fallen to defeat in 1918, but, as historians from Albert Hourani to the more recent (and controversial) Ephraim Karsh have shown, most Arabs had not supported the Revolt in the Desert, led by T.E. Lawrence and his Arab allies, the Hashemite clan of the Hejaz, but their fellow Muslim overlords, the Ottomans. So, what we have in the eventual carve-up of territories, is the classic story of the fall of an old-established empire and the mess and confusion that inevitably happens when such a cataclysmic event occurs.

Britain was in the midst of what Paul Kennedy has described as a severe case of imperial overstretch. There was Iraq to deal with, Palestine, Persia (to protect the oil there against possible Soviet threat), rebellion in Ireland, the occupation of the German Rhineland, and also a growing tide of nationalism now beginning to sweep India, the Raj, Britain's greatest imperial possession.

With *all* this, and Britain semi-bankrupt after fighting the First World War, the maintenance of huge armies in the Middle East, most of whose soldiers wanted nothing better than to go home and to return to civilian life, was a staggering drain on an already highly shaky exchequer. Churchill was fully aware of this, writing to his Cabinet colleague (and former Conservative Prime Minister) Arthur Balfour, that the 'strain of this upon our melting military resources is becoming insupportable'. Financially and in every other respect, Churchill was surely right.

Not only that, but thanks to the mandate system suggested by American President Woodrow Wilson of his brainchild the League of Nations, Britain, like France and Italy, in reality now had an even larger empire than before. Certain territories that had been German colonies or provinces of the Ottoman Empire were now mandates, territories under the legal control of the infant League of Nations but in practice colonies administered as if they were part of the original empires of the victorious allied powers. Britain's included Tanganyika (now Tanzania) and part of the Cameroons, both in Africa, and large swathes of the Middle East.

We think of Churchill as an imperialist. But the cautious fiscal side of him realized, as he told the Prime

Minister, that Britain now had more territory than the country could ever develop, let alone make a profit from.

Britain had seized Baghdad in 1917, having only two years earlier been crushed by Turkish forces. By 1920 the local people were also getting restive about British occupation. One thing is important to remember here: before Churchill created it, there had *never* been a country called Iraq. While it is true to say that two of the provinces, Baghdad and Basra, were Arabic and had much in common with each other, Mosul in the north was quite distinct, and, as one British historian, Peter Sluglett, has suggested, it would have been better if that province had stayed with France and become part of Syria, or the nucleus of an entirely independent Kurdish state.

The rebellion in 1920 was put down successfully but at much cost of life and treasure. To Churchill, Iraq was a major military and financial liability. As he informed his Cabinet colleagues, 'Personally I believe that the military forces in Mesopotamia are out of all proportion to what is justifiable or reasonable to employ in that part of the world.'

In fact, when the rebellion began, Churchill was not even sure whether the newly acquired provinces (finally mandated to Britain by the Treaty of San Remo in 1920) were worth fighting for at all – a retreat to Basra loomed as a possible option in his mind. As he wrote to the British local commander, General Haldane, 'The fate of the province depends entirely on whether a reasonable scheme for maintaining order can be devised at a cost which is not ruinous.' For Churchill – and this is crucial to our understanding of his motives – the new provinces were expense not profit. (While it was known that there was oil in the region, it was not to be discovered until much later on, so Churchill, while aware of oil as an issue in general, could not rely on revenue from it in his calculations.) Saving money thus became his major concern (something also, perhaps, coloured by his aspiration to be Chancellor of the Exchequer).

He informed his Cabinet colleagues that 'prompt and drastic' curtailment of Middle Eastern expenses had to be affected soon, since all in the region was 'ruinous expense'. And, to make matters worse, this was occurring in a 'blistering desert inhabited by a few hundred half-naked native families'. This was of course a major exaggeration. But his basic point was that Britain was expending money and the lives of soldiers in an essentially desert country, neither of which the country could any longer afford. Indeed, as he suggested to Lloyd George, with all the mess going on in Ireland at the same time (Churchill was very involved in the peace talks that led to the founding of the Irish Republic), why Britain 'should be compelled to go on pouring armies and treasure into these thankless deserts' defeated him.

Churchill, although Secretary of State for War and Air, had spent so much time interfering in Middle East policy in general that in 1921 Lloyd George decided to give him the post of Colonial Secretary, a job which, in terms of the turf wars of Whitehall, gave him ministerial responsibility for the Middle East as well. Here Churchill trod on many toes – part of the Middle East, especially Egypt, had been the province of the Foreign Office, and other parts, such as what is now Yemen, were, for historical reasons, under the remit of the India Office. One of his first appointments was to make T.E. Lawrence, the legendary 'Lawrence of Arabia', one of his key advisers.

Churchill knew perilously little about the Middle East, but, as would famously be the case in the Second World War, he was a great sender of countless minutes, memoranda, bright ideas and more besides. One of his first missives was to the great British expert on the Middle East, the very orthodox Sir Percy Cox, in which he stressed again to him, how it was 'impossible for us to throw upon the British taxpayer the burden for military expenditure in Mesopotamia.'

British policy, since the late nineteenth century, had been to have empire on the cheap if possible, and to rule, wherever feasible, indirectly, such as through a native king (as in Africa) or through maharajas, as in India. To Churchill the idea of having a Middle East version of a maharaja or African tribal chief through whom to rule was very appealing, since the nominal ruler could be the front man while the British actually ran the show behind the scenes. In addition, in the post-Woodrow Wilson self-determination climate, it would look as if the new mandated areas were under local administration, while the reality would be different and to Britain's advantage.

Churchill's lack of knowledge about the Middle East made his being in charge and deciding its fate a rather unfortunate prospect, however. He had, for example, frighteningly little idea of what Islam was about. As we know, the majority of people living in present-day Iraq are Shiite Muslims, not Sunni – a schism part-theological and part-political going back to a battle fought on today's Iraqi borders at a place called Karbala, in 680. But Churchill was unaware of this, as we see: 'The

Wahhabi [sic] sect [of what is now Saudi Arabia] is at war with the Sunni. Is it also at feud with the Shia? What are the principal doctrinal and ritualistic differences between the Shia, the Sunni . . . A very brief answer will suffice.'

Here we see the origins of his famous Second World War practice of trying to persuade his officials to tell him everything on one side of a sheet of paper! But how can one condense so much complex history into a single page? Not only that, but as we are sadly now aware, post-9/11, the Wahabi of Saudi Arabia are themselves Sunni, albeit of a far more radical and often intolerant kind, going back to internal reforms in the then region of the Najd back in the eighteenth century.

Churchill decided that the only way to sort things out was to pay a visit to the region himself. Unfortunately he decided not to go to any of the places in which his decisions would make a difference but to Cairo, the Egyptian capital, which its British de facto ruler, the successful liberator of Jerusalem, Field Marshal Allenby, was trying to keep in check. Churchill's visit – that of a very high profile Briton – was bound to cause extra tension on top of all the nationalist agitation that was there already.

Churchill ended up in Cairo with around forty advisers – all white westerners, not locals, and principally British officials. Needless to say, this being the Middle East, Churchill was quick to name them his '40 thieves'! Among them, to the horror of his more staid officials, was T.E. Lawrence, a key member of the Arab Bureau formed in 1916, the British wartime army agency based in Cairo, who now wrote to his family telling them that 'everyone Middle East' was there.

Churchill was methodological in laying out the priorities. He took time to paint and to visit the pyramids, but while he enjoyed himself, this was no holiday. The bottom line, for him, as always, was financial: unless expenditure was cut drastically, there was no chance that Britain could ever hang on in Mesopotamia. Churchill also believed that Britain was *not* out to create a new empire – in fact, to Churchill, some of Britain's African colonies were of more value to the British Empire than its new responsibilities in the Middle East (something fantastic when we now think of the oil riches of that region). Indeed, but for the League of Nations mandate and Britain's obligations under the San Remo agreement, it might be a case of not needing or wanting to be there at all. For him, the solution to the mess and over-expenditure in the region was simple: if Britain were able to get 'an Arab government supported by a moderate military force we may be able to discharge our duties without imposing unjustifiable expense on the British taxpayer.'

So, with cost-cutting in mind, Churchill and his 'forty thieves' convened in one of the most luxurious hotels in Cairo to plot the fate of the Middle East. When it came to choosing a new king, Lawrence and his fellow Arab Bureau member, the archaeologist and Arabist Gertrude Bell, the redoubtable British official based in the Middle East, had no doubts who they wanted – this was Feisal, the unfortunate prince who had fought in the desert with Lawrence during the war, only to be expelled from Syria by the French. He was deemed more suitable than his brother Abdullah, who was fobbed off with Transjordan, now the Kingdom of Jordan, a nation that, unlike Iraq, is still ruled by the descendants of the Hashemite family.

While the experts had their reasons, Churchill was much simpler in why he decided as he did. For him there was one justification above any other: as he told his colleagues back in Britain, 'I have no doubt personally that Feisal offers by far and away the best chance of saving our money.' Feisal was also from outside the country – his homeland of Hejaz was conquered by Ibn Saud in 1924 and forcibly incorporated into the new Saudi kingdom – and, above all, was a Sunni, and therefore not from the predominant Shiite branch of Islam believed in by the majority of those who would now become his new subjects.

Thus, it had to be fixed to look as if the newly-created Iraqi people actually wanted Feisal to come and reign over them: this was arranged, notably by Sir Percy Cox, but with T.E. Lawrence, Feisal's old friend and protector, also playing a part in the subterfuge.

Churchill also decided that the troop levels in Iraq were 'pure waste'. Being always alive to technical innovation, Churchill was swift to realize the importance of the Royal Air Force. Iraq would have its own army and the RAF would remain, far more cheaply, to keep the peace. As Churchill wrote, it was now 'intended to run Mesopotamia like an Indian Native State' – the British High Commissioner would run the show from behind the scenes, as well as keeping an eye on the army. The illusion of local rule and power could thus be maintained, without huge cost to the British Exchequer.

As Churchill put it, the new creation would be notionally independent, 'friendly to Britain, friendly to her commercial interests, and casting hardly any burden upon the Exchequer . . . The Government of the country will be conducted by an Arab administration under King Feisal, who will act in general accord with the advice tendered to him by the High Commissioner Sir Percy Cox.'

This was of course a complete charade. Feisal was no fool, and he realized this fully. Yet, he both wanted to be king – which he knew had to be on British terms – and also to be seen by his new subjects as not being a mere British puppet.

The story of the immensely complex negotiations that followed over the course of the next eighteen months were complex. Churchill was also, as part of his remit as Colonial Secretary, dealing with the equally dire problems of Ireland, and the creation of both the Irish Free State and of the Northern Ireland province of the United Kingdom.

Churchill was determined for Britain to be in real control – as he told his officials, 'we cannot accept the position of Feisal having a free hand' – despite the fact that Feisal was, even if in name only, the chosen king of the new Iraq. But by 1922, he was getting truly fed up of the situation: 'At present we are paying 8 million a year for the privilege of living on an ungrateful volcano out of which we are in no circumstances to get anything worth having.'

By the end of that year the key player in the background, Atatürk, was about to win his final victory – having suppressed Kurds and Armenians alike and driven out the Ottomans, he was now about to get the Greeks finally out of Smyrna (now Izmir) and end thousands of years of Greek inhabitation of the Anatolian plateau, going back to the legendary times of

Jason and the Argonauts, and to the great Byzantine Empire itself.

The sacking of Smyrna in 1922 was to see some of the worst atrocities of the twentieth century to date and the rout of the Greek armies. Massive compulsory population exchanges – now referred to with that horrible euphemism 'ethnic cleansing' – took place. But by the time all this was resolved, by the Treaty of Lausanne in 1923, Churchill was no longer in office. In late 1922 the Prime Minister, Lloyd George, who was, to Churchill's complete despair and horror, totally pro-Greek, argued that the British should stop the Turkish forces at Chanak. This was a step far too far for his Conservative coalition colleagues. Lloyd George was deposed as Prime Minister, never to hold office again. The Conservatives then held and won the 1922 general election.

The solution to the Irish problem – that the Protestant majority six counties in the north of Ireland, in the old Irish province of Ulster, should retain independence – was one in which Churchill had also played a major role. In doing so he gained the confidence of Michael Collins, the IRA leader, who had been very suspicious of Churchill at first (Lord Randolph Churchill had said that Ulster would be right to fight against a united Ireland), but came to see that Winston, unlike his father, was keen to find a genuine and lasting settlement.

As with Iraq, the solution was one that turned out to have major late twentieth- and early twenty-first century ramifications, not all to the good. Churchill's initial thought as Colonial Secretary was massive repression, sending groups of former soldiers known as the 'Black and Tans' to crush Irish dissent by whatever force was deemed necessary, however violent. This failed completely, as the wish of twenty-six of the thirty-two counties of Ireland for independence remained as strong as ever. While Churchill found the 'medieval hatreds' of Catholics for Protestants and vice versa rather baffling, he soon concluded that talks of some kind would be necessary, and that the only way to end the mayhem was to partition the island, with those counties with Catholic majorities becoming part of a new Irish Free State, and the six mainly Protestant counties in the north remaining part of the United Kingdom.

We know in retrospect that this solution would take decades to become workable, if at all, and result in years of violence, as indeed Churchill suspected that it might, since he was fully aware that partition would mean a large Catholic minority residing within the new Northern Ireland, notably in the west of the main city, Belfast, where many Catholics worked in the shipyards. (The Protestant minority in the Free State formed a much smaller percentage, and accepted the inevitable.)

Nonetheless, in 1921–2 it proved the best of the various unpalatable alternatives, and has lasted to this day, despite thirty years of strife between 1969 and 1999 – the 'troubles'. As well as Churchill, the British Prime Minister David Lloyd George was closely involved, and this time the Conservatives went along with the deal, unlike their support of the Unionist rebels in 1913–14. The tragedy was that Michael Collins was murdered by his own side, by members of the IRA who opposed the settlement. The Free State plunged into civil war, but the division agreement held.

With both Iraq and Ireland Churchill certainly did his best, even though, decades later, both those parts of the world broke into conflict of one kind or another. So while the long-term results of his efforts proved unfortunate, he fulfilled his task as well as he could given the exigencies of the time.

In the 1922 general election that followed the collapse of the Coalition Government over the Chanak crisis, Churchill attempted to defend his seat in Dundee, while also suffering from appalling appendicitis. As a result, much of the campaigning had to be done by his wife, Clementine. So when the election was over, and Churchill defeated, along with most of the Lloyd George Liberals, he found himself, as he was to put it laconically later, without a job, without a seat – and without an appendix.

5
IN CHARGE OF MONEY

In 1922 Churchill lost his seat in the general election as a Liberal. In 1924, just two years later, he became Chancellor of the Exchequer, as a Conservative MP in a Conservative Cabinet. He had not only 'crossed the floor' from Conservative to Liberal but he had now reversed the process, a move unique in British politics, and proof that he was never, in any real sense, a good 'party man'. It was an extraordinary transition, caused in part by his horror of Bolshevism after the Communist seizure of power in Russia in 1917, and also by the decision in January 1924 of his old party, the Liberals, to prop up a minority Labour government after the general election of late 1923 had produced an inconclusive result, with no party winning an overall majority. In a by-election to the House of Commons in early 1924 he stood as an 'anti-socialist' Constitutionalist candidate, losing only narrowly to the official Conservative. That same year the Conservative leader Stanley Baldwin abandoned protectionism, and Churchill, a free trader, was able to ally with the Conservative Party he had quit over that issue in 1904.

So when the Conservatives won a large majority in the 1924 general election, and Churchill succeeded in gaining the seat of Epping as a Constitutionalist with their support, the new Prime Minister, Stanley Baldwin, decided to offer him a post. To Churchill's amazement it was that of Chancellor of the Exchequer, one of the top three posts in the Government, and the job he had craved in vain back in 1921 when he was still a Liberal. The British economy, while recovering slowly, was still nowhere near as prosperous as before the war in 1914, and for a free trader such as Churchill to gain such a post from a recently protectionist Prime Minister such as Baldwin was extraordinary, quite in addition to the fact that Churchill had been a Liberal as recently as just two years before.

Churchill's five years as director of the nation's finances are often ignored, since it was not one of the exciting periods of his life. He was neither the young radical he had been during his thirties, nor was he the voice crying in the wilderness against Hitler that he was soon to become. In short, one could say that during this time he was simply a party politician, one given, unexpectedly perhaps, the second most important post in the entire government.

For Churchill this was full circle for the family, and a matter of enormous personal triumph. Two years earlier he had neither seat in parliament nor an appendix, and now he held one of the most important political posts in the country. Not only that, but this was the post his father had held, albeit briefly and ingloriously some forty years before. Churchill had now reached his father's heights, but he was to hold the post for far longer and with much more success than Lord Randolph had ever done, with his ignominious departure in 1887. For Winston Churchill, the party he had rejected in 1904 had now welcomed him back, and to far higher office than his twenty years away from them would naturally have merited. It was, in fact, the most extraordinary comeback imaginable in British politics and he was the surprised and happy beneficiary.

Hindsight, the old saying goes, is a wonderful thing. This applies above all, in his career, to Churchill's decision to put Britain back on to the gold standard, after the United Kingdom had been forced off it during the war, when all the major economies were hit badly. But in April 1925, in his first Budget as Chancellor, Churchill not merely put Britain back on to gold, but to the parity that Britain had enjoyed before 1914, when the old pre-war economy collapsed, at a rate that in retrospect many now feel was unsustainably high. This meant that the pound was fixed, and the flexibility of being off the standard was no longer available to either the currency or to the Chancellor.

The British economist John Maynard Keynes, the vociferous critic of the Versailles peace treaty, and in that period one of the world's leading thinkers on economic issues, felt that sterling, the great imperial currency (equivalent then in many ways to what the dollar has been for the past sixty or more years) was drastically over-valued. This was the era of fixed exchange rates.

Churchill had unintentionally made British industry internationally uncompetitive. Come 1931, and the massive crash in the global economy not seen again until 2007, one of the first things that the new National Government found itself forced to do was to take Britain off the gold standard once again. The six years it spent at pre-war parity had been, in retrospect, a total disaster, and one for which Churchill, as Chancellor of the Exchequer, had been responsible.

Churchill was beginning to wonder about his decision as early as 1927, when he was still in office, and by the time that the Great Depression hit the world in 1931, he was one of the main advocates for reversing his earlier decision. But his fateful first Budget decision had enormous symbolic value that year of 1925, and in making his cardinal error Churchill was in exceptionally good company. Returning to gold after the wartime horrors and near bankruptcy of Britain was seen as what one could call a virility symbol, one that proclaimed to the wider world, on whose trade the country depended, that the days of economic darkness were over, and that Britain and its Empire were now back as key players on the global economic stage.

Not all agreed – John Maynard Keynes, whose views on the economy in general were to be gospel orthodoxy after the Second World War, wrote a searing critique called *The Economic Consequences of Mr Churchill*, a play on his far more famous and influential book *The Economic Consequences of the Peace* on the Versailles settlement of 1919.

The other major criticism of Churchill's chancellorship is his decision drastically to cut back British defence expenditure, and to allow, as Chancellor, the implementation of what is called the 'Ten Year Rule'. This presumed that there would be no major conflict in Europe for the next ten years at least, and, in terms of military spending, that the level of expenditure on defence that had existed hitherto could now be considerably curtailed.

Churchill is often blamed by his detractors for introducing this rule himself, something that Cambridge historian Geoffrey Williams has proved to be technically incorrect, since it was in fact colleagues of Churchill's who created the rule, and as early as 1919, just after the First World War had ended. I would agree with Williams on this point, though would say that in terms of corporate Cabinet responsibility Churchill was equally responsible, as Chancellor, for the decision, and for the way in which it was carried out.

Since Hitler came to power in 1933, and soon began to ignore all the restrictions of the Treaty of Versailles, the fact that Britain's armed services were in no fit state to combat the Third Reich has been one of the biggest criticisms of the British political leadership of the 1930s. The reason our armaments were so paltry in the 1930s was that Churchill had slashed defence spending in the 1920s as Chancellor, the critics point out. And, indeed, there is an extent to which we have to admit that the accusation is sadly true, an admission that brings wrath against the critics from many of Churchill's present-day defenders. He is therefore *technically* guilty. Though, ironically, one of those who would call most passionately for rearmament in the years ahead was, as we shall soon see, no other than Churchill himself. And what *both* critics and defenders often forget is that there is a case for the defence of Churchill as Chancellor based upon what we might call mitigating circumstances.

The other key event of 1925, for which Nobel Prizes were bestowed, was the Locarno Pact, between Britain, France and a seemingly repentant Germany. Sir Austen Chamberlain, now also back in the Cabinet, in his case as Foreign Secretary, was one of the Laureates, and it was a deeply significant event. Germany, under its centre-right chancellor, Gustav Stresemann, promised to honour its western boundaries – in particular those with France and Belgium – and not to resort to war. The event represented Germany's readmission into the global economic and political mainstream. It was now able to join the League of Nations – quitting under Hitler in 1933 – and to benefit from the American decision to help with reparation payments, creating a virtuous economic cycle in which the Germans could pay the British and French, who in turn could repay their debts to the United States, which in its turn could give loans to Germany . . .

The Locarno negotiations happened in October 1925, some six months after Churchill's gold standard budget (and were ratified in December that year). Nonetheless they were very much in the thinking of ministers throughout that period, and Churchill, in cutting back on defence and in agreeing to implement the Ten Year Rule, was going very much with the flow, with the Zeitgeist that said, in effect, that the horrors of war were behind us and that we could now all settle down and enjoy the peace. So once again, while with hindsight he can be seen to be in the wrong, there were an awful lot of other people around him who shared his views.

What no one caught at the time, because the signing of Locarno gave Britain and France such a false sense of security, is that the treaty applied to Germany's *western* borders only, not to those in the east. Remember what happened in 1938 and 1939: Czechoslovakia and Poland, both on Germany's eastern borders, which even in 1925 no German government wanted to recognize as being permanent, were invaded. In fact not until the 1970s, and Willy Brandt's *Ostpolitik*, for which he too won a Nobel Prize, did any German government recognize Germany's eastern border with Poland. So while everyone could jump for joy in western Europe in 1925, the entire Locarno Treaty process was in reality a total illusion, as Hitler was very soon to prove.

Therefore, perhaps the best thing that one can say about the infamous Ten Year Rule, and of Churchill's enthusiastic purging of defence expenditure in order to save the taxpayer money, is that it was right for the time, but that it should have been reversed as soon as Hitler came to power, and the 'Locarno Honeymoon' as the years 1925–33 have been described, came well and truly to an end. This was something that Churchill himself realized, and he spent most of the next six years thereafter trying to do, as he argued for massive rearmament to meet the new circumstances.

It is easy to forget too how much the international scene had changed since 1919 by the time we reached the 1930s. But in the 1920s this could not have been foreseen. In the First World War Italy was on the British side. Mussolini had now taken power there, but right up until the late 1930s there was no reason to suppose that Italy would be a rogue power allied with Britain's enemy,

Germany. Italy did not even enter the war until 1940. In addition, Japan had also been on the Allies' side during the First World War, and in the 1920s the idea that the Japanese would become an enemy was still remote.

In fact, one could argue that the problem in this period is that British Governments were continuing to spend money in the wrong place, because of the vast imperial commitments the country still had. While historians have pointed out that Churchill neglected, for instance, to spend money renewing the Singapore naval base in the 1920s – to his cost, when it fell to Japanese aggression in 1942 – nonetheless the basic problem was that right up until the 1960s Britain suffered from massive imperial overstretch, defending a huge empire in Asia, not all of which could be paid for by the taxpayers of the Indian Raj.

To change this, however, would have entailed an overwhelming paradigm shift in British thinking, something which neither the ruling elite, such as Churchill, nor most ordinary British people, would be prepared to make for decades to come. In retrospect Britain should have cut back on naval spending, concentrated on building a large peace time Army ready to fight on the continent at a moment's notice, and improved nascent fighter capacity in the Royal Air Force rather than building up Bomber Command. All this would have made a complete difference for the better in 1940, but a United Kingdom still living with the imperial mentality of the Victorian era, a country so traumatized by the loss of millions in the First World War, was not the nation to have understood the need for transformative change. This was of course to prove more than costly in 1940, but

Churchill was by no means alone among his contemporaries in being utterly blind to the future that lay just around the corner.

As Chancellor, and as a newly rejoined Conservative, Churchill entered into domestic issues too with enormous gusto, one of which was opposition to the General Strike of 1926. This was when the entire trade union movement brought the country to a juddering halt, with all union members on strike. The Baldwin administration was able both to hold on and also to win. Baldwin was a natural conciliator, and, as opposed to many die-hard members of his party, saw one of his main tasks as bringing the Labour Party, then much more the political wing of the trade union movement than it became in the 1990s, into the mainstream of respectable political life. He also realized that moderates could be persuaded away from the hardliners, and that a bellicose campaign of aggression by the Government against the Trades Union Congress would be tactically unwise.

Churchill, needless to say, was all for as much belligerence as possible! During the strike he persuaded the *Morning Post* to allow its facilities to be used to set up a pro-Government newspaper, which in its brief existence was called the *British Gazette.* Churchill had, as we know, been a journalist, and he now appointed himself editor-in-chief (with Baldwin's sidekick, J.C.C. Davidson, doing his best to calm Churchill down). He wrote much of the newspaper himself, and launched attacks on the striking workers with enormous passion and vim.

As with the miners' strikes in the 1970s and 1980s, the Government regarded the General Strike as essentially political in scope, and thus a challenge to the lawfully elected government of the day: a constitutional issue more than an economic grievance. But Baldwin decided to play this down, and certainly did not see it as an issue over which to call a general election. Churchill, however, saw the whole business in dramatic terms, calling strikers revolutionaries, and, if he had had his way, he would have called in the troops to help run essential services in those parts of the economy where the normal emergency workers were on strike.

Baldwin's tactics paid off. Soon only the more militant miners remained on strike, while all the others went back to work. Baldwin was thoroughly exhausted, so went on holiday to his favourite spa town in France, leaving Churchill in charge of the negotiations.

To general astonishment, Churchill switched tack, and did all possible to persuade the coal mine owners – the mines were not nationalized until 1946 – to make agreeable terms with the workers. So having been a major belligerent, he turned into a conciliator, and this time with success, since he was soon able to settle the strike in a way that kept both miners and coal owners happy.

Churchill was also a Chancellor of the Exchequer who did not forget the country's industrial base, far more at the heart of the British economy then than it is now. As he put it during his tenure:

> I would rather see Finance less proud and Industry more content. [The] fact that this island with its enormous extraneous resources is unable to maintain its population is surely a cause for deepest heart-searching.

He also wrote to one of the major Treasury figures of the day, Sir Otto Niemeyer, the prescient words:

> The Treasury has never, it seems to me, faced the profound significance of what Mr Keynes calls the 'paradox of unemployment amidst dearth'. The Governor [of the Bank of England] shows himself perfectly happy in the spectacle of Britain possessing the finest credit in the world simultaneously with a million and a quarter unemployed . . . This is the only country in the world where this condition exists . . .

In the 1930s fiscal orthodoxy ensured that millions more British working people would be unemployed, and for long periods of time. Churchill was thus prophetic in his analysis of the situation, despite being someone not known for great financial acumen.

In 1929 the Conservatives lost the general election. The Labour Party had the biggest single number of seats – for the first time in British politics – but they did not command an overall majority, depending, as in 1924, on Liberal support in the House of Commons.

As a result Churchill was out of Government office, but nonetheless re-elected as a Member of Parliament, and remained on the shadow front bench until his resignation from it in 1931. He decided to make full use of his newly found leisure, first to embark on a major biographical series on his famous ancestor, John Churchill, 1st Duke of Marlborough, and second to visit his mother's country, the United States. Churchill's realization of the significance in global affairs of the United States, as noted and as we shall see, marks him out as rare among his British political contemporaries; he was one of the few who recognized and understood the enormous potential for good that America could bring.

Churchill's 1929 trip was essentially for fun, however. He met Charlie Chaplin, went to Hollywood, visited Chicago, and also New York and Washington DC, the last being a city with which he would become very familiar in future years. But he also needed to make serious money, since he no longer had the salary of a Cabinet minister, but still enjoyed the lifestyle and spending habits of a great aristocrat (much to his very frugal and thoroughly sensible wife Clemmie's despair). He also had investments in the United States, through his Wall Street financier friend Bernard Baruch. Unfortunately, the prophetic genius that Churchill possessed on future dangers to the British Empire did not apply to his own money, and, along with millions of others, he lost considerable amounts of money in the Wall Street Crash. It was just as well he was so superb a journalist, and so well liked by newspaper editors on both sides of the Atlantic; otherwise he might quite possibly have gone bankrupt, a condition that would have ended his political career, since bankrupts cannot serve in the House of Commons.

The losses of the Wall Street Crash hit Churchill rather badly, without, however, in any way causing him to alter his extravagant lifestyle. It is as well for him that he had a wife as level-headed and pragmatic as Clementine. Soon much of the country retreat he had bought near Westerham, on the South Wolds in Kent in 1922 (and moved into in 1924), called Chartwell, was to be under dustsheets, with only Churchill's study functioning properly. In even keeping such a place, he was living well beyond his financial means, though such a bolthole was to be of much comfort and psychological support to him in the years that followed.

(To leap ahead slightly, another trip to the United States in 1931–2, when he saw his financier Bernard Baruch again, very nearly ended his life altogether. He temporarily forgot that America, like most countries in the world, drives on the opposite side of the road to Britain. He was hit on the streets of New York, though thankfully only sustained comparatively minor injuries.)

Churchill also now began a series of reflective articles on his already amazing life – he was only fifty-five when he lost office in 1929 – that were published in the now defunct *News Chronicle.* These turned out to be hugely successful, and were to form the basis of his bestselling book *My Early Life.* It is extraordinary what he had managed to fit into so comparatively short a lifespan: had he died then, he would certainly have been remembered as a writer, if not for anything else.

However, it is not for his literary output that he was to become especially well known in the decade ahead. The fact of a Labour Government showed that the tectonic plates in Britain were already shifting. One of the new Government's major concerns was to advance the cause of Indian freedom and in so doing they were to arouse the Victorian imperialist in Churchill that was to cast him from any hope of office for years to come.

6

THE WILDERNESS YEARS

One of the greatest myths about Winston Churchill – one that he assiduously fostered himself after the Second World War – is that he was out of office for so long because he opposed appeasement. While he most certainly did reject the appalling and damaging policy of being amenable to Hitler's Germany between 1933 and 1939, he was also against many other policies, including, most notably, independence for India.

In that great classic biography of Churchill by the late Robert Rhodes James, *Winston Churchill: A Study in Failure 1900–1939*, we see all of Churchill's life through the prism of where he was supremely right, in 1940–1, and forget how often his career up until the Munich crisis of October 1938, and his subsequent rescue of Britain from Nazi Germany during the Blitz, was seen as erratic, dangerous and unworthy of high office.

During this period four key themes emerge: India and its progress to independence, which Churchill opposed;

rearmament, which Churchill strongly supported; relations with Mussolini, about which Churchill was ambivalent as long as Italy could be kept on the side of the Western democracies; and opposition to Hitler, whom Churchill opposed with all the possible vigour at his command.

Let us look at how these now unfolded.

In the 1920s, much had been done to further progress towards Indian independence, with talks between various Indian leaders, including Gandhi, and the successive viceroys of India. During the Labour Government of 1929–31 this process was taken much further, so when the Coalition Government came to power in 1931 – an amalgam of Conservatives (under Baldwin), Liberals and a small minority National Labour Party, under the premiership of Ramsay MacDonald – plans were introduced to give India effective home rule, or self-government. To this Churchill was resolutely opposed; he had resigned from the Conservative front bench in 1931, after Baldwin endorsed Viceroy Irwin's proposal of dominion status for India, a year before the Conservatives were back sharing power.

The cause of Indian self-rule was supported by most people of goodwill, across the political divide, and it was only a small and reactionary group of ultra-conservative imperialists who opposed it: a clique with which, over the Indian issue, Churchill now aligned himself. Because of what happened in 1939 – the Second World War – however, we forget that during the 1930s other major events were happening as well as the appeasement of Hitler and Nazi Germany, the debate over Indian independence being one of them. We thus fail to see

Churchill in his so-called 'Wilderness Years' in proper perspective.

People after the war often asked, as they still do, how someone who was so prescient about the Nazi menace could have been ignored when he was so obviously correct. The answer is that the messenger of truth was profoundly flawed. It was Churchill's position on Indian independence and his resignation on that issue which left him outside government, that led to his being ignored when he was right over Hitler and appeasement. The progressive Conservatives around Anthony Eden were horrified at being identified with someone seen as deeply reactionary and as ultra-right wing as Churchill because he was associated with die-hard reactionaries who opposed even the faintest modicum of independence for India. Being close to Churchill branded one, and in the 1930s his brand was not one with which any of the dynamic and ambitious Conservatives in the party, including those who shared his dire misgivings about appeasement, wanted to be linked. In his memoirs Churchill gallantly praises Eden for resigning as Foreign Secretary in February 1938, but at that time the Eden group tried to stay as far away from the contamination of Winston Churchill as possible.

So as we look at his Wilderness Years, we have to remember them in their proper context, of his opposition to appeasement being ignored because of his bull in a china shop reputation, his past failures, such as Gallipoli, and his record of political unreliability, because of having changed parties not just once but twice. As Arthur Herman, the author of *Gandhi and Churchill*, has summarized it:

> The truth is that Churchill's exclusion from influence and power was the direct result of his conduct in the India debates. He had cried wolf for nearly five years, forecasting doom and destruction if the Government of India Bill passed: 'a catastrophe that will shake the world,' he had called it. Then the bill passed and nothing happened. Rarely had a politician been proved so hopelessly wrong, after nearly wrecking his own political party in the process. When he forecast doom again, over Germany, few were inclined to believe him, least of all Conservatives.

The importance of this cannot be exaggerated. Churchill was from the generation that regarded British rule over India as part of the greatness of the Empire, a possession that made the United Kingdom a far superior power to European countries without such colonial strength. To give up India was to abandon the Jewel in the Crown, and would diminish British global power and prestige.

As Churchill put it before the main debates began:

> The truth is that Gandhi-ism and all it stands for will, sooner or later, have to be grappled with and crushed ... It is no use trying to satisfy a tiger by feeding him cat's meat ... [the proposal for Dominion status for India within the Empire. If that happened, Churchill argued, the British Empire would collapse.] That such an organism would pass at a stroke out of life into history. From such a catastrophe there could be no recovery ... The race and nation [the British] which have achieved so many prodigies and have faithfully discharged so many difficult tasks ... [would then become] a victim to their own lack of self-confidence and moral strength.

One of the interesting comments on this speech, made in late 1930, is that of Geoffrey Dawson of *The Times.* As Dawson correctly pointed out, 'The omniscient subaltern of 1896 is not, after all, so very far removed from the statesman who has nothing to learn in 1930.'

Dawson is of course right. Churchill's views are in essence unchanged from that of the brash and bullying young cavalry officer on the North West Frontier of India that he had been some thirty-four years earlier. But how is it that Dawson's name is familiar to us? It is the same Dawson who, as editor of *The Times* not merely supported Chamberlain's appeasement policy a few years later, but also censored out reports from Nazi Germany by his correspondents so as not to upset Hitler and thereby damage Anglo-German relations. By 1937, in the Churchillian canon, Dawson is one of the villains, and since Churchill's opposition to appeasement was morally and strategically correct, rightly so. But here, in 1930, it is surely Dawson who is on the side of the angels, of giving the Indians their long overdue independence.

Thus we see that Churchill's position in the 1930s was far from simple, and that the reasons for his exile from power are not as the myth would have us believe. This was a double tragedy: not only was Churchill ignored over Nazi Germany when he was supremely right, but also, as American historian Arthur Herman suggests, this was the last chance for independence for a united India, Muslims and Hindus together, which would have created a nation that included not only today's India but Pakistan and Bangladesh as well, presuming, that is, that such a nation could have held together.

So it was therefore the India issue that excluded Churchill from office in 1931, since he had resigned from the Conservative leadership in January that year, when still in Opposition. Not only that, but he excluded himself: it was not a case of his being kept out by jealous, lesser beings, as people often presume to be the case.

Churchill might even have seen the India issue as a route to the top, were the Party to be persuaded of his views. However, this speculation is hard to prove one way or the other, but Churchill certainly despised Baldwin, and not without cause, since Baldwin's lack of energy was unquestionably in sharp contrast to the dynamism that Churchill showed throughout his political life – and perhaps hoped to supplant by mobilizing an opposition within the party towards him. But here it is also worth bearing in mind the view of Philip Cunliffe-Lister (later Lord Swinton), the only Cabinet minister of the 1920s and 1930s to whom Churchill gave Cabinet office both in the Second World War and in the 1950s, who argued in his memoirs that the real obstacle to rearmament (and, also, Churchill's political ambitions) throughout the 1930s was not really Baldwin but Chamberlain. It was Chamberlain who became Churchill's great nemesis over appeasement after 1937.

There is however a silver lining to the cloud of Churchill's exile from the National Government in 1931–9: whatever went wrong, as many things did, during that period Churchill bore no responsibility, since he was outside the Government. He was thus able to resume office in 1939 with a clean slate.

In 1935 the India Bill became law, promising a clear route to eventual Indian independence, and Churchill graciously admitted defeat. By this time too the aged and increasingly infirm Ramsay MacDonald, whom Churchill despised as a 'boneless wonder' had stepped down as Prime Minister, Stanley Baldwin replacing him, with Churchill, once more, excluded from the Government.

By 1935 Hitler had been in power for two years, and the nature of the Nazi regime was becoming increasingly apparent, as the frail democracy in Germany after 1919 now vanished under one-party rule. No one could have any illusions about what kind of regime Hitler was running.

As the leading British historian Richard Holmes has so rightly written, Churchill 'almost alone . . . saw that Nazi Germany was unappeasable.' Yet while it is true that Churchill, post-1933 and Hitler's rise to power, knew that Britain had to rearm, he did not understand what it was that the country now needed in order to fight modern war. In this Churchill was not alone, and at least he grasped that *something* drastic needed to be done to improve the nation's defences. Churchill knew that the Royal Air Force needed massive expansion: though it is arguable that even he did not see that fighters were as important as bombers, and that without fighters the enemy bombers would, as Baldwin so feared, always manage to get through. Nor, despite being a Navy expert, did Churchill understand the need for escort ships, or the vital necessity of aircraft carriers, two vital misunderstandings that were to cost Britain dear come wartime.

But, above all, those historians who feel that it was an army as much as an air force that Britain needed in the 1930s are correct in arguing that Churchill, a traditionalist to his core, never understood the need for Britain to have a large army, ready to go at a moment's notice to fight on the continent. Had Britain possessed such a force in 1939–40, the battle for France could have gone very differently, and thus the whole course of the war. To defeat a large land army – like the *Wehrmacht* – one needs a large army in return, and it would not be until 1944, when the Americans landed precisely such a force on continental Europe after D-Day that the scales were truly turned. This not even Churchill, with his profound knowledge of military history, was able fully to grasp.

Nevertheless, while he should have argued from the backbenches for a bigger army, Churchill's campaign to increase Britain's air strength now got under way, and was to last through to the war itself. Yet, here too his pre-1935 opposition to Indian independence, and his reputation as a warmonger, meant that his clarion calls for the obvious were frequently ignored by those who should have listened.

We should also remember how very pacifist Britain was during this time, and not without cause. The Labour Party, for example, which strongly agreed with him in opposing fascism, was profoundly pacifist, especially under the leadership from 1931–5 of George Lansbury, for whom any course to war was unthinkable. It is possible to exaggerate this: the impact of the infamous Oxford Union Society debate, in which the undergraduates decided that they would *not* fight for King and Country, was perhaps untypical. But no one before the First World War had seen carnage and death in any British war such as that on the Western Front in 1914–18.

Not even the Napoleonic Wars had seen such proportionately high death tolls. In 1919 millions had returned from the mud and slaughter of Flanders with the words 'Never Again' in their minds, and now here was Churchill arguing for the exact opposite: war against Nazi Germany.

As we all now know, post-1940, he was exactly right: Nazism, not to forget its allies in Italy and Japan, was a foe so evil and terrible that it *had* to be opposed, come what may. But after the millions of deaths in the trenches, the British people were like the proverbial ostrich, with their heads planted firmly in the sand. Churchill's words were truth, but a message that the traumatized survivors of the First World War did not want to hear.

Nor too did the Chiefs of Staff, and for quite different reasons. As Sir Michael Howard has shown in his highly influential *The Continental Commitment*, the three service chiefs envisioned a nightmare scenario in fighting Germany, Italy and Japan simultaneously, as Britain had interests in all three regions: Europe, the Mediterranean (with the Suez Canal route to India) and the Far East. Fighting a three-front war was simply well beyond British capabilities – we should not forget that in the First World War, Italy and Japan were on Britain's side against Germany, and yet that conflict bankrupted the country as well as costing millions of lives.

Subsequent historians have also shown that the whole imperial commitment of Britain was lethal to the British economy. Imperial orthodoxy believed in defending not only the home territory of Great Britain but the vast empire upon which the sun never set, but the logistics and expense of doing so, especially during a major world recession, were quite horrific.

So while in retrospect Churchill was both morally and strategically right to oppose appeasement and its entire works, there was a kind of rationale behind the policy of the Government, however mistaken. Ordinary people did not want another carnage like the First World War, and the politicians, generals, admirals and air marshals knew that Britain was painfully overstretched and unlikely to be able to fight a three-enemy war. It was the combination of these two things that led to appeasement, and all the dire consequences of that policy throughout the 1930s.

And with politicians always following the popular mood as they weigh their chances of re-election, it is not surprising that the policies of MacDonald, Baldwin and later Chamberlain did everything possible to avoid war. Perhaps the only thing that can be said of Chamberlain is that, unlike the lazy Baldwin, he *actively* pursued appeasement, and genuinely believed in it, but the results were to be even more disastrous as a result.

This is the background to the mess in late 1935 that caused the resignation of the Foreign Secretary Sir Samuel Hoare, over the craven British surrender to Italian aggression in Ethiopia, which Italy had invaded as revenge for Ethiopian victory over Italian invaders nearly forty years before at the Battle of Adowa. Instead of sticking up for Ethiopian independence, as Britain should have done under League of Nations rules, Hoare had conspired with the French Foreign Minister (and later pro-Nazi traitor) Pierre Laval in the Hoare-Laval Pact, which recognized most of Italy's conquest of

Ethiopian territory. Hoare had to resign, and was replaced by the hope of the progressive Tories, Anthony Eden, who, thanks to Churchill's wartime ascent to the leadership, would have to wait another twenty years to become Prime Minister, with disastrous effect, in 1955.

In April 1935 Mussolini, Laval and the British Prime Minister, Ramsay MacDonald, had met at the town of Stresa to reaffirm Austrian independence (which Italy regarded as an issue of national self-defence) and the borders of western Europe agreed at Locarno back in 1925. This became known as the Stresa Front, and was designed to keep Mussolini on side against Hitler, remembering that Italy had been against Germany in 1915–18. This was a not unrealistic policy and although Churchill was firm in his dislike of dictators, being amenable to the Italians was a course with which he himself agreed. He had in fact met Mussolini in 1927 – he was to be glad later that he had never met Hitler – and like many British people at the time he was not completely opposed to what he saw.

Indeed, in 1937, when the appalling Italian invasion of Ethiopia was effectively finished – the Italian air force did not hesitate to use modern weapons with hideous effect against barely-armed locals – Churchill was able to write of Mussolini, possibly with his tongue in his cheek as he did so, that:

> It would be dangerous folly for the British people to underrate the enduring position in the world which Mussolini will hold; or the amazing qualities of courage, comprehension, self-control and perseverance which he exemplifies.

In many ways this is nonsense. Mussolini was all bombast and no substance, so when Italy finally did join Hitler in 1940 it was a fiasco from the beginning, with disasters in Greece and north Africa that the Germans swiftly had to make up, as we shall see. During this same time, Mussolini was also actively supporting his fellow fascist General Franco in the Spanish Civil War of 1936–9, in complete breach of League of Nations demands for outside powers to remain neutral. Mussolini was a seriously nasty piece of work, yet the policy of appeasing Franco could have made sense: despite aid from Hitler (such as the infamous bombing of Guernica by the Luftwaffe) Spain nonetheless refused to side with the Third Reich against the West when war broke out (and Franco thus survived until 1975, dying peacefully in his bed as dictator of Spain).

The appeasement of Italy too could have worked, and Churchill was among those who realized this. So Churchill was not against *all* appeasement, but was totally opposed to any kind of appeasement with the real menace to European peace and international morality, Hitler and the Third Reich. Churchill's prophetic stance on the German issue can best be seen in a speech he made on 16 November 1934 (reproduced in full in Richard Holmes' masterly study, *In the Footsteps of Churchill*):

> I am afraid that if you look intently at what is happening towards Great Britain, you will see that the only choice open is the old grim choice our forebears had to face, namely whether we shall submit or whether we shall prepare. Whether we shall submit to the will of a stronger nation or whether we shall prepare to defend

> our rights, our liberties and indeed our lives. If we submit, our submission should be timely. If we prepare, our preparations should not be too late. Submission will entail at the very least the passing and distribution of the British Empire and the acceptance by our people of what ever [sic] may be in store for the small countries [of Western Europe] . . . within and under a Teutonic domination of Europe.

And to those anti-fascists in the Labour Party who still insisted both in opposing Hitler but also, fantastically, in *reducing* armaments, he had this to say:

> This truth may be unfashionable, unpalatable and no doubt unpopular, but, if it is the truth, the story of mankind shows that war was universal and unceasing for millions of years before armaments were invented or armies organized. Indeed, the lucid intervals of peace and order only occurred in human history after armaments in the hands of strong governments have come into being, and civilization in every age has been nursed only in cradles guarded by superior weapons and superior discipline.

To Churchill two things were needed: massive rearmament and action through the League of Nations, the latter being on the basis that 'peace must be founded upon preponderance', an alliance of good countries against the bad.

In essence, Churchill did not waver from this argument in the years leading up to the war. In addition, from the career of his ancestor the Duke of Marlborough as Captain-General, he understood the importance of alliances like almost no one else. As he put it later on in the pre-war debates:

> For the first time in centuries we are not fully equipped to repel or retaliate for [sic] an invasion. For an island people that is astonishing. Panic indeed! The position is the other way around. We are the incredulous, indifferent children of centuries of security behind the Royal Navy, not yet able to wake up to the woefully transformed conditions of the modern world.

Whether or not the British people were indifferent is moot: in the East Fulham by-election to the House of Commons in 1933, victory went to an outright pacifist candidate, and this, combined with Baldwin's terror of a future enemy bombing campaign against Britain in which thousands of civilians would die, created an atmosphere in Britain singularly unsympathetic to Churchill's point of view. It was not until after the 1935 Labour Party conference, when the robust British trade union leader Ernest Bevin saw the pacifist George Lansbury deposed and the First World War veteran Clement Attlee put in as Labour leader instead, that the policy of funk finally began to lose momentum in a way that would help Churchill in his efforts.

William Manchester, an American writer whose books on Churchill are well known and revered, has expressed astonishment that events within Germany itself – the Röhm Purge in which Hitler had thousands put to death, the banning of free organizations and much more besides – did not wake the consciences of ordinary British people. It is possible that they did not, but it is equally likely, as other biographers have suggested, that while they *did* eventually awaken the consciousness of the left, the majority of British people remained as frightened as ever at the prospect of another carnage in which millions of British soldiers would die in combat and civilians in enemy air raids. While Churchill reflected the bulldog mood of the average Briton in 1940, the feeling in the 1930s was very different.

Since the Nazis and the causes of the Second World War are perhaps the most heavily studied in history, much of what follows will be familiar, including the sad litany of failed chances to stop Hitler when Britain still had the power so to do. The most famous of these missed opportunities was in March 1936, when Hitler, in flagrant disobedience of the Treaty of Versailles, sent the Germany army into the neutral zone of the Rhineland, the area that had been occupied by French troops after 1919, and which was still demilitarized under the terms of the Treaty. Hitler only sent in a small number of troops, just in case there was opposition, but both Britain and France stayed silent, many British people taking the sanguine view of Lord Lothian, the diplomat, that all Hitler was doing was marching into his own 'backyard'.

Churchill realized, however, that this was nothing of the sort, recognizing it for what it was, a surrender to the most brutal ruler in Europe. Give Hitler an inch, he would demand a mile, and events over the next three years proved Churchill's prognosis to be right and right again. As Churchill put it in his memoirs, Britain, instead of persuading France to stand up to Germany, did nothing more than give the French a 'velvet carpet for retreat'. So horrified was Churchill's mole, or secret informant in the Foreign Office, Ralph Wigram, at events that he committed suicide later that year.

While this was going on, even Baldwin realized that it was important to have within the Cabinet someone whose job it was to co-ordinate British defences. Up until that time, each of the services had its own representative in the Cabinet: the Secretary of State for War, the First Lord of the Admiralty and the Secretary of State for Air. Now there was to be a Minister for Co-ordination of Defence: not a single ministry but someone who was supposed to take a wider, multi-departmental longer overview.

Churchill had held all three of the service offices, and was far and away the best person possibly qualified for the post, by virtue both of experience and seniority. But the post went instead to a government lawyer, Sir Thomas Inskip, a leading light in the evangelical wing of the Church of England, and someone without any experience whatsoever of any of the key issues involved.

This was, therefore, perhaps as Baldwin had intended it, a major slap in the face for Churchill, the great expert being passed over for a complete nonentity. (Churchill never forgave Baldwin but he did forgive Inskip.) Churchill had, incredibly, hoped he would get the post. But, a combination of political grudges, memories of his disastrous failings in 1915, and, as we know from Churchill's memoirs, the policy of appeasement held against him. If he had been appointed, it would have been perceived, so the British political establishment thought, as a major provocation to Hitler so soon after the invasion of the Rhineland. So Churchill, who would have known what he was doing, was passed over.

However, as Churchill was to realize himself, this was just as well, since he continued to have no responsibility for the disastrous policies that ensued. As he put it, this 'was not the first time – or indeed the last – that I have received a blessing in what was at the time a very effective disguise'. He was completely free to attack the Government for its appeasement of Hitler and for its woefully late and inadequate rearmament policies, and thus able, as noted, to enter office in September 1939 entirely untarnished by what had gone before.

There is one point, however, made by acute observers such as Hugh Bicheno and Richard Holmes: how much difference would it have made had Churchill got the job? In one sense, it would have been huge, had his colleagues allowed him to proceed with full-scale rearmament. But in another, the change would not have been as much as one would suppose. For they argue that Churchill was a great defender of the air doctrines of the founder figure of the Royal Air Force, Lord Trenchard. As we will see, the doctrine of the primacy of the bomber was in fact a chimera. Bomber Command slaughtered thousands of German civilians during the war, but failed completely to strike the hammer blow against the Reich that would have given the victory that they held could be won by aerial bombing alone. Churchill was as much part of the bomber school of thought as its guru Lord Trenchard, and so was among those who failed utterly to realize that the only way to beat Germany was to have an army on the field big enough to take on the *Wehrmacht*. Therefore, while we can and should cheer Churchill for doing exactly the right and unpopular thing to do – urging the Government to rearm against the Nazi menace –

nonetheless the awkward fact remains that it was essentially *the wrong kind of rearmament* for whose lack Churchill was so eloquently attacking the supine National Government of 1936–9.

1936 also saw a now legendary exchange between Churchill and Baldwin on the issue of defence, one that led to the famous index entry in the first volume of Churchill's war memoirs: 'confesses putting party before country, 169–170'.

The East Fulham by-election in 1933 unnerved Baldwin, who had thus not encouraged talk of rearmament until after the general election two years later. This lack of urgency, something that marked Baldwin's temperament let alone his views on armaments, astonished Churchill, who had rightly recognized the international situation as getting worse by the day. As Churchill put it in the debate in late 1936:

> Two things, I confess, have staggered me . . . The first has been the dangers that have so swiftly come upon us in a few years, and have been transforming our position and the whole outlook of the world. Secondly, I have been staggered by the failure of the House of Commons to react against these dangers . . . I say that unless the House resolves to find out the truth for itself it will have committed an abdication of duty without parallel in its long history.

Churchill was exaggerating for effect, but not by much.

Baldwin's response was, thanks to Churchill, to become infamous. In the political context just described, he then said:

> My position as leader of a great party was not an altogether comfortable one. I asked myself what chance was there ... within the next year or two of that feeling being so changed that the country would give a mandate for rearmament? Suppose I had gone to the country and said that Germany was rearming and that we must rearm, does anybody think that this pacific country would have rallied to that cry at that moment? I can think of nothing that would have made the loss of the election from my point of view more certain ... [but as Baldwin delayed] we got from the country, with a large majority, a mandate for doing a thing that no one, twelve months before, would have believed possible.

In other words, vitally needed rearmament was postponed purely for reasons of party calculation ...

In fact, the election of the Labour Party in 1935 would have been much worse since Lansbury, as we have seen, was a conviction pacifist, not one for the sake of Party calculation. But given the scale of the National Government's majority in 1931, the swing to Labour that would have been needed for them to win was surely too high, and Baldwin could easily have risked some degree of rearmament and still been returned with a safe majority. As Churchill was right to note, Baldwin had truly put party before country.

Then, at the end of 1936, out of the romantic nature of his heart, Churchill made another monumental blunder that once again saw his rearmament campaign ignored in favour of another of his quixotic gestures. This was his defence of the feckless Edward VIII and his campaign to marry the divorced American Wallis Simpson. And not only was Edward misguided in this: he was also firmly sympathetic to the Nazis. Consequently, his moral and ideological, let alone marital, unsuitability to be king was obvious to all – except for Churchill.

What Churchill thought he would get out of his support for so evidently flawed a figure is impossible to fathom, since it acted as a catastrophic diversion from the successful cross-party campaign in which he was now also involving himself, the Focus Group, namely that of support for the rule of law in international affairs in a way that could contain the Nazi threat. The *bien-pensants* of the inter-war liberal left were as involved in this group as Churchill, since the earlier mindless pacifism of the Labour Party was now receding. But just as it was beginning to get somewhere, Churchill threw all this away in deciding to come out against Baldwin and the desire of not just the Government but opinion throughout the Empire that if King Edward VIII wanted to marry his mistress that he would have to abdicate as king first.

As Richard Holmes has commented on the 'Abdication Crisis', as it was called, Churchill's foolish intervention marked 'the lowest ebb of Winston's political career. It killed the momentum of the Focus Group and it ruled him out of consideration for political office when Neville Chamberlain became Prime Minister' soon after, in May 1937.

Whether or not someone as seriously blinkered and vain as Neville Chamberlain would ever have given someone as independent-minded as Churchill worthwhile political office is a moot point, as Churchill concedes in his memoirs. Astonishingly, in the light of subsequent events, Churchill actually agreed to a request by Lord Derby, the great Lancashire landowner and Tory grandee, to second the nomination of Chamberlain as leader of the Conservative Party. Churchill was probably being magnanimous, as he was in a private letter he wrote to Baldwin on the latter's retirement. It would do him no good. For as Churchill understood, while Baldwin disliked the world beyond the Channel, Chamberlain, a far more dynamic individual, was under the false impression that he, the new Prime Minister, understood it well and could deal with it. Lloyd George had once dismissed Chamberlain, whose far abler half-brother, Austen, died in 1937, as 'a good Mayor of Birmingham in a lean year'. As soon became apparent and, as Churchill foresaw, this business-like, parochial approach to dealing with a global menace on the scale of Adolf Hitler was to prove an unmitigated disaster.

In 1938 Hitler committed his first act of overseas aggression: the *Anschluss*, or the expressly forbidden unification of Austria, the land of his birth, with the Reich. To Churchill this invasion was an 'outrage', and, as he told the House of Commons on 14 March:

> The gravity of the event . . . cannot be exaggerated. Europe is confronted with a programme of aggression, nicely calculated and timed, unfolding stage by stage, and there is only one choice open, not only to us but to other countries, either to submit like Austria, or else take effective measures while time remains to ward off the danger . . .

Presciently Churchill realized:

> Where are we going to be two years hence, for instance, when the German Army will certainly be larger than the French Army, and when all the small nations will have fled from Geneva [the League of Nations headquarters] to pay homage to the ever waxing power of the Nazi system, and to make the best terms that they can for themselves?

As Churchill knew, Czechoslovakia, the great Central European democracy, was now surrounded by the Third Reich on three sides.

But an event the month before is often overlooked. Anthony Eden, long fed up with Chamberlain's interference, finally snapped and resigned as Foreign Secretary in February 1938. One of his key reasons was Chamberlain's contemptuous dismissal of an offer by the United States President, Franklin Roosevelt, to help mediate in international problems.

In the light of the United States now being the predominant world power, this would today seem fantastic. But then America had long been in isolation, and the Soviet Union was a pariah state because of its Communist ideology. Chamberlain, and many others in the British political elite, therefore effectively ignored both countries.

One person who never made such a mistake was Churchill, who, as we have seen, was not only half-American but also knew the United States well. And one of the many crucial things that Churchill got exactly right in this period was that the sooner the 'Great Republic', the biggest and most powerful democracy on earth, was reconnected to the rest of the world the better.

This realization is perhaps one of Churchill's greatest achievements and one for which he deserves the fullest praise.

Churchill was doing his best to make his campaign non-partisan (unlike the profoundly partisan Chamberlain), as he made clear in a speech in the great Free Trade Hall in Manchester on 9 May:

> I have felt it my duty to make exertions, so far as I can, to rouse the country in the face of an ever-growing danger. This is no campaign against the Government of the day, nor against the Opposition. It is not intended to promote the interests of any Party, or to influence the course of any Election . . . [So] what is the purpose which has brought us all together? It is the conviction that the life of Britain, her glories and message to the world, can only be achieved by national unity . . .

Churchill had been widely attacking the Government for its lacklustre rearmament impetus. In that month he attacked the Air Ministry, and, as one of his biographers, Robert Rhodes James, has suggested, he was unfair on the Secretary of State for Air, Lord Swinton, who was in fact doing his best despite Chamberlain. The Prime Minister used this as an excuse to sack Swinton (who Churchill was later to re-employ in his wartime and later governments) and install the Chamberlainite minister Sir Kingsley Wood as the new Secretary of State. It was an unfortunate episode, and Chamberlain was also able to reject Churchill's plea for a Ministry of Supply, which did not come into being until it was almost too late the following year.

Churchill was now if anything taken more seriously on the left than on the Conservative benches, with the so-called 'Glamour Boys' of ambitious Conservatives still clustering around Eden rather than Churchill. But nothing stopped Churchill from his jeremiads, and, for example, on 2 June he took the battle to Birmingham itself, the heartland of Chamberlain's power. Here he told the meeting:

> The idea that dictators can be appeased by kind words and minor concessions is doomed to disappointment. Volcanic forces are moving in Europe, and sombre figures are now at the head of the most powerful races. The dictator countries are prepared night and day to advance their ambition, if possible by peace, if necessary by war. I am under the impression that we and other countries stand in great danger.

Churchill was more right than he knew. He understood the peril in which the democratic, peace-loving Czechoslovakia now lay, and that a major crisis was about to erupt.

7

THE MAN WHO WAS RIGHT

Churchill's epic *The Second World War* runs to a gigantic six volumes. And it is a hard task to condense into a few chapters the sheer scale of Churchill's achievements – and failures – during that extraordinary period. But Churchill's greatest ever achievement was to save Britain from Nazism in 1940, having been the one major Conservative statesman in the years leading up to the war who fully understood the scale of the Nazi threat, not just to the United Kingdom as a nation, but to civilization and freedom itself. Whatever mistakes Churchill made throughout his sixty and more years in politics, all of them pale in comparison with this supreme achievement. While, as we saw in the introduction, we should not forget his faults because of what he accomplished in 1940, nor should we make the opposite mistake of belittling his salvation of Britain and of civilized values in 1940–1 because he had a distinctly erratic career up until that heroic time.

We saw what he did in 1940–1 in the first chapter. Here we look at the build up to war chronologically in terms of his life. The story itself is so exciting that we must not depart too far from our narrative, but much of the debate about Churchill, for and against him, hinges on those crucial three years 1938–41. So, before we move on to the account of those years, we need to look at how it has been evaluated since.

First, *the heroic interpretation*, mainly stemming from 1940, Britain's 'Finest Hour', and the way in which Churchill's own six volumes created the myth of how the once-despised hero in the wilderness came back to save his country and lead it to inevitable victory.

Then we have *the revisionist interpretation*, mainly deriving from books written in the 1970s and onwards, that shows all Churchill's long litany of mistakes (from Gallipoli onwards), and which argues, in essence, that he threw away British global power by abject and craven surrender to American interests, especially in 1941–5, an extraordinary view to most of us, but one which is actually believed by serious and otherwise thoroughly decent historians. Finally, we have the *warts and all view*, which admits that while Churchill made numerous errors during his unique sixty-plus years in politics, he was, as the heroic school has it, right in 1940 to say that surrender to Hitler was immoral; right to say that without the United States coming to Britain's aid in 1941, not just the United Kingdom but the whole British Empire would have fallen; and, last but not least, that American global predominance had long since been inevitable, and that all Churchill did was to recognize that it would happen regardless.

In other words, from 1933 onwards, *Churchill got it right about Hitler*, and as the Government ignored his prophetic voice, and as Hitler rearmed, his pleas became of necessity all the more urgent.

So now to turn again to 1938, the year in which Britain could have won the war, and, ironically, in the light of the passionate defence of Neville Chamberlain by the revisionists, the only year in which it could have done so *without* American aid.

Nowadays, because we know that the Second World War did happen, despite all Chamberlain's efforts to preserve peace, and because we have all seen pictures of Belsen and the concentration camps, we find it incredible that anyone would want to appease Hitler. But we forget that what the appeasers saw were not the gaunt faces of Jews in Auschwitz, but those who fought in the trenches in what we now call the *First* World War, but what they then called the *Great War*, a conflict so horrible that the like had never been seen before in Europe. (Americans had their Civil War, but this was not considered by statesmen on the other side of the Atlantic.)

Thus, for Neville Chamberlain and his Foreign Secretary, Lord Halifax, the priority was to prevent another war on the scale of the Western Front, and the death and horror of a battle like that of the Somme. And here, one must concede, the revisionists do have a good point in stating that there was thus a strong moral imperative on the side of the appeasers.

But the problem was that Hitler, and the whole apparatus of the Nazi state, was geared for eventual mass conquest and war, as historians such as Richard Evans and Ian Kershaw have demonstrated so clearly from their researches of the archives of the Third Reich. So, however dreadful the trenches of Flanders – and, unlike Chamberlain or Halifax, Churchill had actually served, albeit briefly, on the front line – and however much nice, rational men in the democracies wanted it or not, war with Nazi Germany was inevitable.

And now we come to the final irony of the 1938–9 period: Neville Chamberlain, by throwing democratic Czechoslovakia to Hitler in 1938 destroyed Britain's only chance of getting rid of Hitler without *both the United States and the USSR*.

In other words, the reason why Britain was in so dire a position in 1940, alone against the foe, was entirely Chamberlain's fault. It was he who put Britain in a position in which only the United States could rescue the United Kingdom and its Empire, not Winston Churchill.

Consequently, when Germany seized Austria in an entirely illegal coup in February 1938 – an episode familiar to all viewers of *The Sound of Music* – it seemed eminently reasonable to a businessman type such as Neville Chamberlain that all that was taking place was an unfairly forbidden reunion of ethnic Germans, the *Anschluss*.

So no problem – far from it, as Churchill now understood.

Yet, look at a map from after February 1938 and it is obvious what is at stake: the entirely pro-Western, uniquely liberal, democratic, civilized state of Czechoslovakia is now surrounded on three sides by the hostile forces of the Third Reich, from the south in the former Austria as well as from the west and north in Germany. Not only that, but all the country's superb fortifications, natural mountain defences, and armaments factories were in the part of the country directly contiguous to the newly expanded Reich. And in that same area, the Sudetenland, lived most of Czechoslovakia's German minorities, a legacy from when Bohemia had been part of the great Austrian Empire after the Battle of the White Mountain in 1620.

Once again, to the rational businesslike Chamberlain, it was understandable that Hitler would want the ethnic Sudeten Germans to be reunified with their ethnic kin over the border in the Reich. It was only fair, after all . . .

But Churchill was not an expert on the history of war, and on his ancestor's epic campaigns, for nothing. He saw what few in the West understood, but what others, from democratic Czechs to the Stalinist Soviets saw only too well, that once the Sudetenland was given up to Hitler, Czechoslovakia would, in a stroke, be rendered entirely defenceless against future – *and inevitable* – Nazi aggression. All their natural mountain defences, all their fortifications, and the internationally famous Skoda Works (the best weapons factory in Europe) would all fall into Hitler's grasp. Democratic Czechoslovakia would be utterly betrayed to a savage tyrant.

Stalin, and his then comparatively moderate Foreign Minister, Litvinov, saw this too – and here, historians are now realizing, was the *huge* blunder by Chamberlain that made war inevitable. For Stalin was enormously upset at events, and began the process of listening to the hardliners in his government, notably Molotov, who suggested to him that the West was unreliable and that the best way forward for the USSR was to make a deal with Hitler to protect their own interests. A dictator-

dictator deal now began to brew, and a power struggle for Stalin's favour within the Kremlin commenced behind closed doors.

Chamberlain had the extraordinary habit of putting top secrets into the open post letters he wrote most weeks to his maiden sisters. They give his innermost thoughts – and are therefore a gift beyond measure to historians. In one, he confessed to a profound distrust of the USSR – and in another to thinking that the Americans, the world's biggest democracy, were good for nothing but words. So, in September 1938, he eventually agreed to see Hitler, near the dictator's holiday home in the German province of Bavaria, and then to go to a meeting at the German capital, the city of Munich.

Here, with Mussolini (for Italy) and Deladier (for France), the four powers agreed that all the borderlands of Czechoslovakia – the Sudetenland – would be given to the Third Reich. Since most of the people living in these border areas were ethnic Germans, Hitler could maintain that he was simply reuniting his own people. But with all the Czech defences and key armaments factories in these areas, Czechoslovakia was left all but defenceless. Not only that, but the poor Czechs themselves, and the Soviets, had been ruthlessly excluded from the Munich settlement, a betrayal that the both the Czechs and the Soviets felt very deeply.

We can understand why the Czechs felt betrayed. But the exclusion of the Soviets is just as important, and, in the months to come, was to have the direst of consequences, as Churchill was well aware.

Why was this so important? Let us first look at the all-important context and then return to our narrative.

Until Gorbachev's brief rule of the former USSR, Western historians laboured under the severe disadvantage of having no access to Soviet Union archives, which remained sealed and closed to prying Western eyes. This resulted in a totally distorted vision of the past: we knew what Britain's, the United States' and France's positions were, and what Hitler was thinking, but had no idea of the internal politics of Stalin and his cohorts in the Kremlin. There was speculation, but it was no more than that. Then Gorbachev allowed historians in, and overnight our picture of the pre-war years was transformed: finally we knew what the Soviets were *really* thinking and a full history of that era could be written. As a result we discovered, through the works of Jonathan Haslam, Gabriel Gorodetsky, Michael Jabara Carley and others, that the Munich Conference of 1938 was an even worse disaster than we had known.

We already knew that the Czech defences were some of the very best in Europe, and German generals, interrogated after 1945, confirmed this. Poland, to whose defence the British went quixotically in 1939, had an antiquated army and no natural defences to speak of. Consequently, Britain soon discovered, the *Wehrmacht* was able to conquer Poland in days. This, the German generals understood, would have been impossible with a far better defended Czechoslovakia, with far superior armed forces, and natural defences that the *Wehrmacht* were right to fear. The conquest of Czechoslovakia would have been far more costly to Hitler than the walkover a few months later in Poland.

Up until the Munich agreement, made between Britain, France, Italy and Germany, and from which

Chamberlain was to exclude the Soviets, Stalin remained open to his comparatively moderate Foreign Minister Litvinov's support for the idea of collective security. He was still ready to deal with the West – provided, of course, that the West was prepared to deal with him. This was something that Churchill understood fully, and Stalin knew this because the Soviet Ambassador in London, Ivan Maisky, kept Stalin fully in touch with the internal British debates on the issues of the day.

And here, on the need to involve the USSR, Churchill linked himself with the Labour Party, something that in itself spoke volumes. For no one had been keener than Churchill back in 1917–22 to invade the USSR, to side with the White Russians against the Bolsheviks, and to strangle the infant Soviet Union at birth. Churchill, the great anti-Bolshevik, was now the principal British politician arguing passionately in favour of involving the USSR in the international political system and creating an anti-fascist front in which they would be a full participant.

However, with the betrayal to Hitler of the Czechs, and the exclusion of the USSR from all diplomacy, Litvinov's position within the internal Soviet debate was rendered untenable – he was lucky to keep his life in the purges then raging in Moscow, in which hundreds of thousands were liquidated on Stalin's orders. The Soviet leader now switched sides, making Molotov the new Foreign Minister, and, at a point on the exact timing of which historians still disagree, decided that the best course of action for the USSR was to do a temporary deal with Hitler, that would buy time for the Soviet Union, either by letting the Western capitalist countries go to war with each other, or by allowing the USSR to build up its strength, or perhaps even both.

The result of this was the infamous Molotov–Ribbentrop Pact of August 1939 (sometimes also called the Nazi–Soviet Pact), in which the two dictatorships signed a deal not to go to war with each other. We also now know that Hitler and Stalin also carved up much of Central Europe between them, with eastern Poland going to the Soviets and western Poland to the Germans, and other parts of Europe being similarly apportioned.

This meant that that when Hitler went to war in September 1939 he did not have to fear what the Soviets would do – he had, in effect, bought them off. This made the subsequent conquest of Poland, and then of western Europe, far easier, and it was, one can argue, a major contributor to the fall of France in 1940. France had in theory been an ally of the USSR, as had Czechoslovakia, but with Chamberlain excluding the Soviets in 1938, Stalin saw no reason to aid France in 1940.

As a result, while Chamberlain was greeted with popular acclaim by the people in London when he returned from Munich in 1938, in fact, in acting as he did over Czechoslovakia, he had guaranteed the war that he had been so anxious to avoid. Not only that, but he had made certain that when it was fought, it would be considerably more disadvantageous to Britain when it began, so much so that the country came, regularly, within a hair's breadth of losing the war time and again between 1940 and 1941. This, we now know, was Chamberlain's fault, and, as Churchill foresaw precisely, was completely avoidable.

So while Chamberlain is a tragic figure, as his defenders claim, the new evidence is even more in Churchill's favour than before, and the picture of a voice crying in the wilderness is actually truer than even Churchill himself could have imagined, since he did not know what the Germans feared about the Czech defences or what the internal debates were in the Politburo in Moscow.

Churchill's speech in October 1938, after the betrayal of the Czechs at Munich, in which he claimed that the policy that led tens of thousands to cheer Chamberlain in the streets (a popularity we should not forget, however inconceivable it would seem to us today) was a disaster, is still worth repeating:

> I will . . . begin by saying the most unpopular and most unwelcome thing. I will begin by saying what everybody would like to ignore but which must nevertheless be stated, namely, that we have sustained a total and unmitigated defeat, and that France has suffered even more than we have.

He was right of course: but at the time his was still a minority view, and had Chamberlain done as some of the party leadership wanted and called a sudden election, it is likely that Churchill might not even have been re-elected. He was heckled during his speech by those who proclaimed that Chamberlain had brought peace but continued:

> All is over. Silent, mournful, abandoned, broken, Czechoslovakia recedes into the darkness . . . [Since

> 1933] all the opportunities of arresting the growth of the Nazi power . . . have been thrown away . . . [The British Government] neither prevented Germany from rearming nor did they rearm ourselves in time . . . What I find unendurable is the sense of our country falling into the power, into the orbit and influence of Nazi Germany, and of our existence becoming dependent upon their good will or pleasure . . . And do not suppose that this is the end. This is only the beginning of the reckoning. This is only the first sip, the first foretaste of a bitter cup which will be proffered to us year by year unless by a supreme recovery of moral health and martial vigour, we arise again and take our stand for freedom as in the olden time.

One thing has been known for some time, and it is also to Churchill's merit. On 15 March 1939 the Germans invaded the rump Czechoslovak state. The western half became the Nazi-ruled protectorate of Bohemia and Moravia, and Slovakia became a Nazi puppet state. There were no ethnic Germans in either place, and the lie of Hitler only wishing to expand to reunite separated Germans was exposed. Churchill had, once again, been proved right.

And, just as important as the gaining of territory, the Germans were now able to seize the Czechoslovak army's equipment, having already taken over the legendary Skoda weapons works the previous autumn. When France was invaded a year later, hundreds of tanks and armaments used by the *Wehrmacht* were actually Czech. The munitions of a democratic pro-Western ally were thus used by Hitler's Germany in its successful conquest of western Europe, thereby negating the claims of the appeasers that by delaying the war from 1938 until 1939 helped the West gain time.

(It should also be pointed out that while Britain was able to rearm in 1938–9, so too were the Germans, as American historians like Telford Taylor have been able to show. Not only that, but Britain had also lost both Czechoslovakia and the USSR as allies on the anti-Nazi side of the balance of power, and that loss massively outweighed any gain in time the country might have made in March to September 1939.)

Despite the collapse of his appeasement policy, Chamberlain resolutely held to office after March 1939. Churchill continued to be excluded, despite growing press clamour to have him restored to office. Chamberlain and Lord Halifax now decided that they would, after all, give guarantees against Nazi aggression to Poland, Romania and Greece, none of which were democracies, and, in the case of Poland and Romania, were countries that were also physically impossible for Britain and France to guarantee. Not only were they geographically inaccessible, but both were also terrified of the USSR, since they had gained much territory at Soviet expense after 1918. With the USSR effectively now an enemy rather than a friend, their situation was truly hopeless – yet it was to them that Chamberlain gave his promise, and one that would compel Britain into war at a time now of Hitler's choosing, since the Nazi dictator was bound to make one of those countries his next conquest.

Chamberlain did finally agree to desultory talks with the USSR, sending Britain's delegation, under the splendidly named Admiral Sir Reginald Plunkett-Ernle-Erle-Drax, not by plane but by boat. (France also sent a negotiating team.) But Poland was able to have veto rights over what Britain and France could concede, and compared to the German delegation's earlier offer, which gave Stalin half of Poland's territory, was really no competition.

Despite the imminent onset of war, there was still a major lack of seriousness about the British Government. Conscription, for example, so vitally necessary for war, did not come into effect until September 1939. Not only that, but the British Expeditionary Force – the army ready to serve in France – was still miniscule, despite the fact that in order to win the previous war, the biggest ever conscript army in history had been necessary. British military doctrine was still stuck in the nineteenth century, the lessons of the First World War totally unlearned if not actually discarded; though, as we shall see, much of Churchill's own concept of strategy was equally anachronistic, if not eighteenth-century, the age of his great ancestor the Duke of Marlborough.

On 1 September 1939 the anticipated German invasion of Poland began, matched, to the horror of that country's Western allies, by an equally brutal Soviet invasion from the east. Britain's belated guarantee to Poland came into effect, and, as a result, on 3 September 1939 the United Kingdom – and its Empire – found itself again at war, for the second time in the twentieth century. Finally, and at long last, Winston Churchill found himself back in office, as First Lord of the Admiralty, in political charge of the Royal Navy. His wilderness years were over.

The irony is that although Churchill was at a ministry directly connected to the conduct of the war, it was in the same office, literally and metaphorically, that had nearly torpedoed his career during the First World War.

Churchill's second tenure at the Admiralty was to be, militarily speaking, as disastrous as his first, with the catastrophe of a failed invasion of Norway in 1940 substituting for the Dardanelles. However the effect on his political career was to be the exact opposite – whereas he thought he was permanently sunk in 1915, the result of the Norwegian debacle was to propel him to the top office, the premiership, twenty-five years later.

Alas, Churchill had brought with him many misunderstandings and a lack of appreciation of new naval technology that were to cost the Royal Navy very dear, both short term in Norway and long term during the rest of the war. First, he did not understand the vulnerability of destroyers to aircraft attack – we shall see why this was catastrophic come 1941. While Churchill had been instrumental in creating the Royal Air Force, he did not grasp that all the naval guns in the world could not protect even the best battleships from sustained aerial attack. Secondly, he did not fully comprehend how vital escort discipline was in naval convoys, again a serious error come the need to keep Britain going with supplies, especially after 1941.

His views, in short, were those of another age, and while his romanticism about Britain and its great island story was to be of inestimable value after May 1940, in terms of how to fight contemporary warfare his antiquated beliefs made him dangerous in command.

Perhaps the biggest disaster of this period was what the Americans aptly called the 'Phoney War', when Britain and France effectively did nothing in terms of military offensives *directly against Germany itself*. As we all know, the French sat behind the Maginot Line of defences with Germany, and the RAF dropped leaflets not bombs over German soil.

This was, of course, the fault of Neville Chamberlain, and, it should be said in fairness, his equally supine French allies. Inactivity almost seemed a basic article of faith! From this we can exempt Churchill altogether – which was both a good thing and a catastrophe. For while the British and French governments sat behind their defences in lethal lethargy – they believed that Germany could be brought down by economics rather than military action – Churchill busied himself with ways in which the Germans could be engaged, at least somehow.

The method he chose, the peripheral approach, would remain his favourite strategy for much of the war, once more with dire results, even after the United States entered the war in December 1941, following Pearl Harbor. It had been at the heart of British military thinking for centuries, and reflects the fact that the United Kingdom and its Empire was, at least until 1914, primarily a naval power. Britain traditionally did not fight major wars upon the continent – we forget, when looking at the campaigns of Marlborough and Wellington that many of the troops that they successfully commanded were not entirely British, but were drawn, throughout the centuries, from the armies of Britain's continental allies. This was how the British Empire did war: it had the Royal Navy, and a small continental force, while its allies carried out the bulk of the fighting on land.

The First World War had changed all this – the tiny British Expeditionary Force of 1914 ended up becoming the biggest army that Britain had ever seen. The days when the United Kingdom could rely on the Prussians against the French, or the French against the Germans, were over. However, in 1939, it was as if the First World War had never been, because Britain had a comparatively tiny army and a Royal Navy as powerful as ever. Not only that, but, again unlike the First World War – in which Britain had engaged the enemy more closely but in this case on land – this time the main plan against Nazi Germany ruled out a direct attack by British and French armies against their enemy on German soil.

So Churchill had to come up with alternative strategies, not just to keep the show on the road, but also to combat the masterly inactivity of his colleagues. And thus he chose, as Britain had in previous wars, the peripheral approach.

His first idea was to launch a Naval campaign in the Baltic Sea, a brainwave he had enjoyed in the previous war, but one that all his advisers were as resolutely against as their predecessors had been. So that notion was thankfully dropped.

The second one – a campaign in Scandinavia – was a new idea, and, unfortunately for the poor Norwegians, was one that Churchill was able to launch.

Some background is needed here. In 1939, the Soviet Union invaded hitherto neutral Finland. This rightly outraged opinion in the West, which also had a strong element of anti-Bolshevism to it. Churchill had been, correctly, a zealous proponent of doing a deal with the USSR against Hitler, as we have seen. But after the

August 1939 Pact, which brought the Soviets and Nazis together as, in effect, allies, carving up Poland between them and, in the Soviet case, sending massive war material, including oil from the Caucasus, to help the Third Reich, all Churchill's old anti-Bolshevism returned, and he became one of those who, fantastic as it may seem today, actually advocated going to war with the USSR *as well as* Nazi Germany. This would, of course, have been more than catastrophic had it actually occurred. But in 1940 this was considered very seriously by both the British and French governments, and it was only the common sense of Turkey, a neutral country, in refusing Allied planes permission to fly over Turkish territory to bomb the Soviet oil fields at Baku (now in Azerbaijan) that stopped such a disaster from taking place.

All this, however, drew Churchill's attention to Scandinavia, and to the fact that both Norway and Sweden, two neutral states, were supplying Germany with much needed war material, especially chrome. Consequently, he developed the idea of mining the seas around Norway to stop supplies from getting through, even though this was a serious breach of Norwegian neutrality. (He would cheerfully have invaded Sweden as well, given half a chance.) This might seem drastic, but such was Churchill's choice, with dire results.

In February 1940 a German ship, the *Altmark*, containing British prisoners of war, was raided, and the captives were freed. This move was understandable, but what happened next was a mistake.

The Royal Navy, under Churchill's auspices, now decided to mine the approaches to Norway, and planned landings on Norwegian soil to follow. By now the Finns had surrendered to the Soviets – having in the meanwhile put up a magnificent resistance against overwhelming odds. So at least the wild notion of going through Norway to Finland to help the latter was now off the table. But on 5 April Churchill's Norwegian scheme began.

Disaster swiftly followed. The Germans now invaded both Denmark and Norway, not to ensure supply routes but to conquer them for the Third Reich. British troops had scarcely landed than they had to flee, in ignominious retreat, with large amounts of invaluable supplies having to be left behind. Not only that, but Norway was to give the Germans the opportunity to begin atomic weapons research, a dire development only prevented by brave British and Norwegian special forces destroying the heavy water plant at Telemark later in the war. Churchill's bright idea had only strengthened Hitler, not diminished him.

Naval historians, especially Stephen Roskill, who wrote the official account of the Norwegian campaign, have rightly blamed Churchill for his blunders, especially for his micromanagement, a fault he was to exhibit time and again as the conflict progressed. Two good things did emerge though, which, while not excusing Churchill, did help considerably both quite soon and also later on.

First, Churchill realized that, as in the Dardanelles fiasco, inter-service planning and coordination was dreadful – indeed non-existent. So when he became Prime Minister in May 1940 he also made himself Minister of Defence, with a personal senior staff officer,

General Sir Hastings 'Pug' Ismay, to ensure what we would now call joined-up government. This was to make running the war considerably easier, though it did not, alas, altogether remove inter-service rivalries.

Also, Hitler remained convinced that Churchill would again try to attack Norway. In suspecting that Churchill did indeed *want* to do this, he was entirely right: Churchill would press for *Jupiter*, as the planned Allied attack on Norway would be code-named, throughout the war. It never happened, but, as Paul Kennedy has rightly pointed out, several German divisions were stationed needlessly in Norway throughout the war, uselessly holed up near the fjords waiting for an invasion that never came. They would otherwise have been deployed against Allied troops in Normandy, and would have made the liberation of Europe harder and costlier. So there was a long-term silver lining to the Norwegian cloud.

There was a short-term benefit as well. While Britain was expelled from Norway, the Royal Navy was, nevertheless, able to wreak considerable damage to the German fleet, such that, come June 1940 and the evacuation of the British Expeditionary Force from the beaches of Dunkirk, German naval forces were in no position to enter the Channel to prevent it from taking place.

However, the most extraordinary outcome of the Norwegian fiasco was the most amazing of all. In the First World War, the Dardanelles catastrophe had seriously damaged Churchill, but this time, the debate on the Norwegian debacle in the House of Commons in May 1940 was to result in his becoming Prime Minister.

In the debate, in which Conservatives such as Leo Amery joined the Labour and Liberal parties in opposing the Government, Churchill did his best to defend the Prime Minister, since it was his own personal responsibility that so much had gone wrong. But most Members of Parliament knew that while Churchill was technically guilty, he had been out of office during the entire appeasement period, and thus in a wider sense not at all responsible for the mess in which Britain now found itself. In particular, Neville Chamberlain did not help himself during the debate by playing partisan politics, since it was clear that a consensus was now emerging that Parliament wanted a cross-party coalition government to run the war.

Theoretically Chamberlain won the debate of censure, which took place on 9 May. But his majority was seriously slashed, with numerous Conservatives either voting with the Opposition, or abstaining. Chamberlain tried to use the excuse of Hitler's invasion of the Netherlands and Belgium to stay on, but the Labour Party refused to serve under him. He therefore had to go.

With the benefit of decades of hindsight, we may presume that Churchill's premiership was now inevitable. However, in doing so we would be wrong. Britain nearly had the Foreign Secretary, the Earl of Halifax, as the next Prime Minister, which would, as Piers Brendon and Richard Holmes, among others, have pointed out, have been a terminal catastrophe. With Halifax as Prime Minister, Britain would not have fought on alone – the country would have surrendered to Hitler, before the United States could engage in the war, and thus have been subjected to possibly decades of Nazi tyranny and worse. (Robert Harris's famous novel (and the film) *Fatherland* would have been fact, not fiction.)

The Conservative Party and the Court, led by George VI and his wife, Queen Elizabeth, favoured Halifax. The Labour Party would have accepted him and worked with him. But thankfully for the future of Britain, democracy and freedom, Halifax felt that being Prime Minister, apart from giving him stomach ache at the very thought, would be impossible for him as a member of the House of Lords. So when he, Chamberlain and Churchill met, Halifax refused. Chamberlain thus had to recommend Churchill to the king, and it was Winston Churchill who George VI appointed as the new Prime Minister on 10 May 1940.

8
THE ATLANTIC ALLIANCE

Churchill's realization that military salvation would come from the United States is as much part of his outstanding achievement in saving Britain in 1940–1 as his oratory, his dynamism, his keeping Britain fighting and his sheer will to survive.

This was seen by 1941, when the situation was already improving, with Roosevelt doing all he could to help Britain short of actually going to war. In January the President sent over his chief factotum Harry Hopkins and initiated Lend-Lease. This meant much needed weaponry for Britain, with payment after the war. It was a huge help, but as John Keegan has reminded us, 'Lend-lease was, however, only a means of playing for time. Though it kept Britain in the war, it did not bring victory any nearer . . . The future looked grim indeed.'

Churchill remained profoundly grateful to the United States, later recalling Lend-Lease as one of the 'most unsordid acts in history'. He told the Americans in 1941: 'Give us the tools and we will finish the job.' He knew by how small a thread British survival hung, and that anything that the United States could give, on whatever terms, might make all the difference, the margins being as scarily narrow as they were.

In fact, only active US intervention could really change the course of the war, however many destroyers Britain could obtain from the United States. The decision in Congress to introduce the kind of military conscription needed to fight a war passed, it must be remembered, by a single solitary vote – it could, as Roosevelt was aware, have gone the other way – and the President, however solid in support he personally was for the British and for the principles of democracy and freedom, never forgot that the isolationist spirit was very much alive in the United States right down to Pearl Harbor (and, as books by those such as Pat Buchanan have shown, to this day, there are Americans who feel that getting involved in the Second World War was a mistake, however much of a minority view this is and was.)

British people tend to forget this – the British *survived* alone but *did not win* alone. As Richard Overy so rightly points out in his book, *Why the Allies Won*, they won because the world's biggest industrial superpower, the United States, unleashed its full economic might in creating an army and its hardware that Germany and Japan came nowhere near being able to match, in part because American soil itself was never invaded by its enemies. America was, as it has been nicknamed, the arsenal of democracy, and this is something that

Churchill fully understood, however old-fashioned he might have been in many ways.

Churchill's revisionist critics in Britain have condemned him for, as they see it, selling the family silver to the United States. However, one needs to ask, how else could Britain have survived at all? Britain had no other option and Churchill knew it. Survival is always a price worth paying, and whatever the cost to the United Kingdom's imperial pride, one must surely come to the conclusion that Churchill made absolutely the right decision.

In August 1941, after the Nazi invasion of the USSR, Churchill sailed on the *Prince of Wales* to meet Roosevelt, the first of many meetings that these two men would have through the course of the war. The meeting, in Placentia Bay, Newfoundland, was actually in Canada, a country at war with Germany. Churchill made a major faux pas by forgetting that he and Roosevelt had actually met before, during the First World War, when the President was still a comparatively humble Assistant Secretary of the Navy. Roosevelt had found Churchill arrogant, a 'stinker . . . lording it over us', but now Churchill was the unimportant one, a besieged British politician begging aid from the most powerful man in the democratic world.

Thankfully for all concerned, the second meeting went well. Roosevelt was able to push through the Atlantic Charter, a ringing endorsement of freedom and democratic values: as Churchill had argued earlier, this was not just a war against the Axis, but one for the very basis of civilization itself. There was nothing concrete in the Charter that would compel the USA into the war, but in its endorsement of democracy and of peace, one could say that there was at least some kind of statement that showed the war to be about principles and not just old-fashioned power struggles. There was, however, an American sting in the tail: if all peoples were to be free, what did this say of the millions under British colonial rule, most notably in India but also throughout the British Empire as a whole? This was to cause much aggravation between the two leaders later on, with Roosevelt unable to understand why Churchill so resolutely refused India its independence.

One of the British military officials at the meeting, Colonel Jacob, lamented that he did not find any of the American armed services keen to go to war on Britain's behalf. The strain of isolationism that had so tragically kept the world's biggest democracy out of world events for twenty years still ran strong in many parts of the United States, despite all Roosevelt's heroic efforts.

There was however one very good piece of news that was to make enormous difference to Britain once the United States finally did enter the war later that year. This was that the United States, if war came, would put the defeat of Germany first. This is something many take for granted, especially if they are British. But it was in fact a major step taken by the American army, and one in which it would frequently come up against the serious dissent of the US Navy, whose personnel were often not merely Anglophobes, but also strongly favoured putting the struggle against Japan first instead.

Indeed, if one considers that what propelled the United States into the war was Pearl Harbor, a Japanese attack, against the US Navy, then it is all the more remarkable that the Americans kept their August 1941 promise to Churchill, since there were very powerful voices, not just in Washington DC and the navy but throughout the country that wanted revenge against Japan given the top priority. One could say that it was an act of monumental foolishness by Hitler that saved Britain, since in declaring that Germany was at war with the United States after Pearl Harbor, he set America at war with the Third Reich.

The decision to make Germany the priority had already been decided by one of the most underestimated military leaders of the Second World War, someone whose role is certainly ignored in Britain in comparison with the military commanders in the field, such as MacArthur in the Pacific and Eisenhower in Europe. This was General George C. Marshall, the US Army Chief of Staff, and the man who Churchill was later to admit was the true organizer of victory. Before Roosevelt and Churchill had even met, Marshall, and his planning staff, who included a promising younger officer named Eisenhower, had put together a Victory Plan. The defeat of Germany was to be the priority when war came; and it is thanks to Marshall and his cohorts that the United States stuck to this, despite massive pressure from both the navy and a vengeful American public to fight Japan instead.

So on 7 December 1941, the day of the attack on Pearl Harbor, a day that Roosevelt told the American people would always 'live in infamy', Britain, thousands of miles away, was to be saved at last. Churchill's dream of the United States' entry into the war had come true, and as he was to recall later, he was able now to say, 'so we had won after all!'

Wartime coalitions are notoriously hard things to run. The Grand Alliance – the joining and coordination of forces of the United States, and Britain, and, in a slightly different way, the Soviet Union, against Nazi Germany and Japan – as Churchill called it, would prove to be no exception, as he would increasingly discover.

When Hitler carried out his act of greatest folly – the invasion of the USSR in June 1941 – Churchill was able, as he had been during the 1938 Munich crisis, to put behind him decades of anti-Bolshevism, and declare that the Soviet Union was an ally in the struggle against Nazism which he would do all possible to help. When he told his young secretary Jock Colville this, he was surprised, but Churchill countered that, 'if Hitler invaded Hell, I would at least make a favourable reference to the Devil in the House of Commons.' Ideologically, this was a major change for Churchill, the old anti-Bolshevik but, as we have seen, he had been advocating better relations with the USSR back in 1938, only to be ignored on this as on so many other things by Neville Chamberlain. Germany was the main enemy for him, and anyone who would fight the Third Reich was Britain's friend, whatever that ally's ideology.

As Churchill broadcast to the British people (here including parts of the speech usually left out):

> The Nazi regime is indistinguishable from the worst features of Communism. It is devoid of all theme and principle except appetite and racial domination. It excels all forms of human wickedness in the efficiency of its cruelty and ferocious aggression. No one has been a more consistent opponent of Communism than I have for the

> last twenty-five years. I will unsay no word that I have spoken about it. But all this fades away before the spectacle which is now unfolding. The past, with its crimes, its follies and its tragedies, flashes away. I see Russian soldiers standing on the threshold of their native land, guarding the fields which their fathers have tilled since time immemorial . . . And then my mind goes back across the years to when Russian armies were our allies against the same deadly foe . . . I have to make the declaration . . . We have but one aim and one irrevocable purpose. We are resolved to destroy Hitler and every vestige of the Nazi regime . . . Any man or state who fights on against Nazidom will have our aid . . . This is our policy and that is our declaration. It follows, therefore, that we shall give whatever help we can to Russia and the Russian people.

So in June, Britain and the Communist USSR became allies, and in December the Grand Alliance became a threesome, with the might of the United States coming to the rescue. But with this, as writers such as the historian Norman Davies, in his vitally important book *No Simple Victory: Europe at War 1939–1945* (also called *Europe at War 1939–1945*), and similarly BBC television documentary maker Laurence Rees, in his series (and book) *World War II Behind Closed Doors: Stalin, the Nazis and the West*, have shown, the war became morally ambiguous.

This goes against all we have been taught about the Second World War, and its status as a 'good war', a morally clear conflict between the Allies, the good guys in the white hats, and the baddies, the Axis, in the dark hats. But such a clear dichotomy was in fact not the case, and it was something that Churchill, by 1944 at least, realized himself, which is why the final volume of his epic work on the war is called *Triumph and Tragedy*.

Let us remind ourselves of the casualty figures of the Allies: around 300,000 deaths in total for the United States and the United Kingdom combined, and between 20 and 27 *million* for the USSR. There is no real comparison. Hundreds of thousands of deaths are truly terrible, and the suffering of Britain during the Blitz, and the later V-rocket attacks were dreadful, as survivors know. But in the USSR *millions* of people died, soldiers and civilians alike. The suffering of the Western Allies, such as Britain, Canada and the United States, does not even approach that of the Soviets.

Not only that but, to remind ourselves again, 85 per cent of German casualties were on the Eastern Front, in the war between the USSR and the Third Reich. Only 15 per cent of German deaths were incurred during battles against the West, in Italy and north-west Europe. We like to think that D-Day made a difference, whereas the truly epic battles against Hitler were those such as Kursk or Stalingrad.

This is why those who say that, in effect, the USSR won the war in Europe and the United States that in Asia are right. This is in no way to belittle the huge sacrifice of immensely brave British soldiers, seamen and airmen in all the different theatres of war – far from it. But it is to put it in perspective, something that those in Britain may not like to hear, and which Churchill himself found increasingly unpleasant to realize as the war progressed, and as he found himself ever more unimportant in relation not just to the United States but to the USSR as well.

The Alliance also brought a very different moral slant to the Second World War, as Churchill despairingly came to understand. If you live in the United States or the United Kingdom, then the outcome of the Second World War is indeed a very good one – the triumph of civilization over barbarity. If you live in Italy, France or the Netherlands, say, then the basic feeling remains the same, notwithstanding that in the course of liberating these nations from Nazism the Allies had to flatten towns, causing the deaths of many civilians who had been on their side. Despite this, liberation did bring true release from tyranny, and western Europe soon found itself both free and protected against its new foe, the USSR, by the might of the United States.

However, if you live in Central Europe, especially, say, in Poland or Czechoslovakia, then it is a very different story altogether. For in these two countries, and others in the region, six years of Nazi tyranny was replaced with over forty years of alien Soviet tyranny and despotic rule from Moscow. That is why the Churchill speech quoted earlier is so perceptive: Churchill knew that *morally speaking* there was no difference at all in barbarity between the USSR and the Third Reich. Stalin had been allied in all but name to Germany in 1939–41, and by the time that *Barbarossa* came, Stalin had killed far more of his own people in the purges than Hitler was ever to kill in the Holocaust. The statistics tell all: 6 million Jews murdered by the Nazis, 20 million Soviets killed by their own government.

For millions of people, therefore, the Second World War did not bring a happy outcome but decades of further suffering, that only ended in 1989, fifty years after the war had begun, when the Iron Curtain collapsed. For them, therefore, the moral benefits of the conflict are distinctly ambiguous, and the victory did not bring the clear-cut ending with which we associate it – with good cause – in the West. Just as Churchill did not, those of us in the West should not forget this, and neither should we forget that as many Soviet and German troops died in a single day on the Eastern Front as the total number of Allied servicemen on the Western Front throughout the entire war.

So in 1941, Churchill's moral dilemma was indeed a profound one, as he knew, but for the sake of keeping Britain safe, he had no choice but to ally with Stalin. As time went by, though, the Faustian nature of this pact would become ever increasingly apparent, and be the tragedy alongside the triumph when the war ended four years later in 1945.

On Churchill's first visit to Washington DC in December 1941, to see the Americans, and to plan the future of the war, there were, however, no moral ambiguities: the world's greatest democracy was coming unequivocally to the aid of its British ally, and with the strategy of defeating Germany first still very much in place.

What is amazing is that the Soviet–United States–British Grand Alliance managed to keep going throughout the war. We take this for granted, but, as Churchill knew from the campaigns of his ancestor the Duke of Marlborough, wartime coalitions did not always survive a conflict.

Nor should we forget that while the two nations were democracies, the United States and the United Kingdom did not always see alike on everything. Most Americans were with Britain every inch of the way on the war, especially in the cause of defeating someone so palpably evil as Hitler, but the maintenance of the British Empire, especially the Raj in India, was another matter altogether. While the Anglophobia of the US Navy was often quite marked, even some of those in the Army, such as the great General Patton himself, had distinct feelings of superiority to the imperialist Britons with whom they now served. While it is true that Americans pursued their own interests – as any country would do – it is also surely true that American might was bound to prove the greater of the two countries. This was not always easy for Churchill to grasp, and, on many issues, he would fight with Roosevelt for a different policy if he thought Britain's position would suffer.

The new Chiefs of Staff grouping, with Sir John Dill, the British Army's Chief of the Imperial General Staff (CIGS) of 1940–1, as the effective military ambassador in Washington DC from 1941 with the title of Head of the Joint Staff Mission, worked superbly well throughout the war, not least because Dill was rightly regarded very highly indeed by both Marshall on the American side and Dill's successor as CIGS from 1941, Sir Alan Brooke, on the other. Things were not always smooth, but the regular and now formalized links between British and American armed services made decision-making and execution a huge amount easier than would otherwise have been the case. For his part in setting this up on the political side Churchill deserves full credit.

Richard Holmes' biography of Churchill rightly summarizes this phase of his life as 'centre stage', and the years afterwards as being 'supporting role'. The logistics of this are quite simple. Up until late 1943 most troops in the field were still from Britain and the Empire (Canada, Australia, New Zealand and India). Thereafter, the large majority were American, and this gave the United States far more say in how things should be run. So until then Churchill was, to use a British political phrase, able to 'punch above his weight'. Thereafter this was no longer possible, especially after the United States began to establish bilateral relations with Stalin, and not to Churchill's advantage.

In 1942 Churchill was able to get his way with Roosevelt, as successfully as Britain was losing badly in the field, losing Tobruk to Rommel and the vital Navy base of Singapore to the Japanese, with both short-term and post-war catastrophic results for British power and prestige in Asia.

The loss of Tobruk was embarrassing, as it happened when Churchill was on one of his visits to Washington DC. The fall of Singapore, and the capture into brutal captivity of so many British, Australian and Indian troops cut Churchill deeply. For a brief while he was criticized as never before in the House of Commons, and there were even fleeting plots, soon put aside, to have him replaced as Prime Minister. Historians have rightly condemned Churchill for not seeing to the Singapore defences much earlier – the guns faced the wrong way round, for example – but the truth is that, as we saw earlier, Britain was grossly overstretched and profoundly over-committed, having to defend the homeland against a still possible German invasion, fight the *Wehrmacht* in North Africa, and then defend the vast Asiatic empire against the Japanese.

There was no possible way in which a country as limited in its economic and industrial resources as the United Kingdom could possibly have been able to defend as much as was required by a war against three enemies simultaneously, as the Chiefs of Staff had predicted accurately in the 1930s. Not until 1967 did any British government grasp this, so in this error Churchill was not alone. But it gave him much temporary embarrassment in 1942, and it was the realization by the ruling elite that no one could do the job of Prime Minister as well as he could in wartime that saved his political skin.

That year saw many meetings on both sides of the Atlantic, too many to recount in a brief biography. But as Richard Holmes helpfully reminds us:

> During the war Winston and FDR exchanged more than 1,700 letters and telegrams, on average nearly one a day. They also met in person ten times, eight of them at bilateral meetings and the other two with Stalin, spending a total of 120 days in each other's company. History records no comparable association between the leaders of two major nations.

This is indeed the case, and one should remember that transatlantic journeys were far more difficult then than they are now, even if they were made by plane. Even General MacArthur, no Anglophile, said that Churchill deserved a medal for his brave travels by air in wartime conditions. Thankfully for both specialists and general readers, the entire wartime correspondence between Churchill and Roosevelt has been published, in several volumes, allowing us an insight into their collaboration as we can read the numerous telegrams, letters and notes they sent one another as the war progressed.

Both leaders were larger than life characters, from privileged patrician backgrounds, and also men very confident in their own opinions. One thing was different, however, and that was the fact that Roosevelt did not micromanage operations on the Churchillian scale. He was often happy to leave details to his subordinates, sometimes playing them off against each other in ways they would find disturbing.

There was one time Roosevelt sided with Churchill against his own soldiers, and that was over the issue of where US troops should fight first in 1942. Discussions took place on both sides of the Atlantic: on one side of the Atlantic, between Churchill and his service chiefs and US Army Chief of Staff General George C. Marshall, Roosevelt's key aid Harry Hopkins and the US Army Department's up and coming star and expert military planner Colonel Dwight D. Eisenhower; and on the other side of the Atlantic, the same people, plus Roosevelt and other key American personnel.

We can see the meeting through the eyes of Stephen Ambrose, the American historian now famous for his book *Band of Brothers* (also an internationally acclaimed television series of the same name) about US troops fighting all the way from Normandy to Bavaria. What he says, in an essay in the book *Churchill* edited by the British historian Robert Blake and his United States counterpart William Roger Louise, on the Marshall–Hopkins–Churchill–Brooke talks is significant:

> This remains one of the great controversies of the war. Churchill and his supporters insisted that the Allies were in no way ready for a 1943 cross-Channel attack. They pointed out that landing craft were insufficient, that the Allies had not yet won mastery of the skies over France, that American divisions still needed training, that the *Wehrmacht* was too strong. Eisenhower and the Americans insisted that a 1943 invasion would work and would lead to a quicker end to the war. They pointed out that there were sufficient landing craft for two major invasions in the Mediterranean, that German defences in France (the Atlantic Wall) would be twice as strong in 1944, that if airpower used in North Africa, Sicily and Italy were stationed in England in 1943 mastery of the air over France could be won, that German tank, aircraft and artillery production was increasing and would peak in 1944, and so on.

And Ambrose concludes on the issue of *Roundup* (known by 1944 as *Overlord*) in 1943:

> In other words, for every argument why a 1943 invasion of France could not work, there was a counter-argument. We will never know, as *Roundup* was never tried. What did happen was exactly what Eisenhower feared . . .

Military strategists and historians have disagreed with the decisions made in 1942 ever since, sometimes, alas, with much ill-will on both sides. In the end, for good or bad, Churchill was able to postpone D-Day until 1944 and, as Max Hastings has demonstrated conclusively, he was nervous about it even then.

It is important to remember that the discussions were not just about tactics, but also about essential strategy:

what was the best way to defeat Hitler, the enemy whom both sides fully agreed was the main foe, to be defeated first, before then going on to deal with Japan. So, the arguments were not simply about what to do, how, when and where, but also conceptual, with each side having a very different philosophical and strategic approach on how to win not just this war, but in fact any war.

For Churchill, his Chiefs of Staff, and for centuries of British soldiers and military leaders, the key to victory was the peripheral approach. This had worked for Britain time and again, and made sense for the reasons given earlier: Britain's limited resources of money and manpower, and the consequent priority given to obtaining primacy of the seas, achieved through the power of the Royal Navy. In the early years of the war, as we have seen, while Chamberlain effectively did nothing against the Germans until Hitler took the initiative in 1940, Churchill was able to attack the Reich, albeit indirectly, in North Africa and through bombing. Better Churchill's indirect approach and *doing something*, it can be argued, than Chamberlain's view – with which Churchill was not entirely unsympathetic – that Germany could be brought down by blockade alone, and *doing nothing*.

The United States' approach to war was entirely different: *hit the main enemy direct and go for the shortest available route to victory.* In the case of the Victory Plan put together by Marshall and Eisenhower, this involved attacking Germany head-on in north-west Europe, and preferably in 1943, a plan they gave the operational code-name *Roundup* (now known as *Overlord).* Marshall was an outstanding logistics expert – a vital field which, as Sir Basil

Liddell Hart has commented, was not Churchill's greatest strength – and he was able to put together a detailed programme of how the United States would have enough troops and landing craft to launch a direct invasion of Europe in April 1943, one year from when he, Hopkins and Eisenhower first came with their plan to England. Not only that, but Roosevelt signed off on the plan as well, thereby defeating those admirals in the United States who had wanted to put Japan's defeat ahead of that of Germany.

Unfortunately, there was also a side-plan, code-named *Sledgehammer*. This was designed for launch in late 1942 if the Soviet Union collapsed, and if, therefore, Germany was wining the war in the east against the USSR. (These code-names can be confusing. We need simply to remember that *Roundup* became *Overlord* when put into effect in 1944, on D-Day, and that the other plans were contingencies if the USSR surrendered.)

This side-plan proved to be a mistake. Any invasion in 1942 would have to be accomplished primarily with British and Canadian troops. The British generals, with strong memories of the slaughter on the Western Front 1914–18, of which they were understandably traumatized survivors, immediately foresaw a massacre of First World War proportions, and one that would be, if the attack were made in 1942, almost entirely of British and Commonwealth forces.

However, what Churchill and his generals failed to understand was that if the invasion took place later – in 1943, as Marshall wanted, for instance – the overwhelming number of troops in action would then be American not British. Indeed, D-Day was effectively speaking almost the last day of the war in which British and American troops on the field were equal – thereafter, as we shall see, the vast majority of soldiers fighting in Europe were to be American.

Not only that, but the United States was the greatest industrial power on earth, and had so huge a manufacturing capacity that it very swiftly overwhelmed anything with which the Axis could compete. This meant, as Eisenhower and Marshall knew, that the United States' war capacity was of an overwhelmingly greater magnitude than anything the far smaller Britain and its old, white Dominions Commonwealth could ever imagine producing. While it made every possible sense for the United Kingdom to adopt the peripheral approach, especially against so comparatively powerful an enemy as the Third Reich, the same strictures did not even remotely apply to the United States, which was far stronger than Germany on its own, let alone in alliance with the United Kingdom, Canada, Polish exiles and Free French.

So, in summary, while *Sledgehammer* was completely – and understandably – unacceptable for Britain, *Roundup*, with the all-powerful United States in charge, was to Marshall and Eisenhower the obvious, least costly, fastest way to knock Germany out of the war.

It is worth adding here that there has been confusion in the work of some recent historians over the discussions surrounding *Roundup* and *Sledgehammer*. American archives show very clearly that Marshall and Eisenhower planned for D-Day to be on 1 April 1943, and there is no ambiguity about this. They also show that *Sledgehammer* was only to come into operation if the

Soviets lost or were in imminent danger of total collapse. It was, in other words, a contingency plan, *and nothing else*. The full-scale invasion that Eisenhower and Marshall wanted, and upon which Roosevelt signed off, was always *Roundup*, and that was for *1943* (as the American writer, Stephen Ambrose, famous for his book *Band of Brothers*, always understood correctly).

Churchill was ambivalent about when Britain could in fact land troops in France. On the one hand, he insisted he was open to what the Soviets called the 'Second Front', an attack against Germany from the west to match the visceral and titanic struggle between the Third Reich and the USSR in the east. On the other hand, he remained solidly wedded to the British peripheral strategy throughout the war, and was always coming up with new and exciting possibilities of fighting the Germans almost anywhere *except* head-on in north-west Europe. And, as Churchill's personal Chief of Staff, General Ismay told Marshall's biographer Forrest Pogue, the 60,000 casualties Britain suffered on the first day of the Battle of the Somme in the First World War was forever at the front of the minds of Churchill and his generals whenever they listened to American plans for boldness and direct assault upon Germany.

Marshall went home thinking that he and Eisenhower had prevailed, and that the British were fully signed up for his plan to go into northern France in 1943. It did not take him long, however, to find that he had been deceived and that, in reality, the British opposed *both* plans, his main 1943 invasion scheme as well as the much riskier *Sledgehammer*. Needless to say, he was furious and, for a while, contemplated siding with his rival,

Admiral King, and the US Navy, and putting the war against Japan first, the Pacific over the Atlantic. Thankfully for Britain, this anger proved fleeting, and, in any case, Roosevelt insisted that Germany remain the main enemy however hurt Marshall's feelings.

Away from the talks, Churchill was having a terrible year. In December 1941 the Royal Navy had lost two of its best battleships to Japanese bombers in the Pacific – Churchill never fully grasped that ships could be vulnerable in this way. Then, in 1942, came one of the worst disasters in the history of the British Army – the fall in February of the Singapore garrison to the Japanese, with thousands of British and Australian troops and civilians taken prisoner, many to the most appalling and inhumane treatment in degrading prison camps.

Many things have been said about the fall of Singapore, which was a major blow to British prestige in Asia from which, it has been argued, the Empire never fully recovered: a defeat of soldiers of European ancestry by an Asian army. It has also often been said that Singapore fell because the guns were facing outwards – in expectation of a seaward attack, rather than landwards – because Britain and Australia simply never expected the Malayan peninsula, through which the Japanese invaded, to fall so rapidly to enemy assault. All this is true, as well as the comment by Correlli Barnett, the former Churchill Archivist, who points out that Churchill had so invested his armed forces in the Middle East, fighting the Germans and Italians there and in north Africa, that all other areas, included Singapore, were denuded of vital resources.

However, while Churchill cannot avoid his share of the blame – he had never agreed to the extra fortifications needed better to defend the Singapore naval base – the issue is in fact more complex. As we saw in the 1930s, the Chiefs of Staff were terrified of the United Kingdom being at war simultaneously with Japan, Germany and Italy – something that politicians like Chamberlain used subsequently to appease the dictators and avoid such a war. But by 1941 the military nightmare had come true, since Britain and its Empire was indeed simultaneously at war with all three opponents.

No one was a more zealous defendant of the British Empire than Winston Churchill – indeed, during the war some British troops were in India suppressing the independence movement rather than fighting the enemy. But he had to put defence of the British Isles first, and this is precisely what he proceeded to do. So while he was indeed culpable for losses in the Pacific, it is also the case that Britain did not even begin to have the resources to fight an effective global war *on its own.* Churchill, in his desire to see the United States enter the war, understood this, even though, as we shall see, he did not always grasp all its ramifications.

The very simple fact is that the Chiefs of Staff back in the 1930s were right: the United Kingdom was grossly overstretched, and the simultaneous defence of *both* Britain *and* its Empire was impossible. The defence of home soil had to come first, with the consequence that there were losses to the Empire in Asia such as Singapore, Malaya and Hong Kong, all of which fell to the Japanese.

So Churchill was both blameworthy, on the one hand, and a man who had no real choice, on the other. Nor was he alone in the fond delusion that Britain should be able to defend both itself and its Empire, since it was not until well into the 1960s that the British finally withdrew from east of Suez, after Churchill himself had died. In reality, it was only the United States that could fight two-front wars, of the kind successfully fought against the Germans in Europe and Japanese in Asia. The United States had the resources and Britain did not.

In July 1942 there was a motion of censure against Churchill in the House of Commons triggered in the main by anger at the fall of Singapore. Thankfully for him, the rather inept proposer – an obscure backbench Conservative – reduced the House of Commons to laughter by suggesting that George VI's brother the Duke of Gloucester be made Commander-in-Chief. After this blunder Churchill was safe, but it does show how depressed the British as a whole, let alone the political class, had become by the saga of one defeat after another.

For the year 1942 saw both major defeats and final victory for the British forces in north Africa. In June, when Churchill was conducting delicate negotiations with Roosevelt in the White House, the news came through that Tobruk had fallen to Rommel's forces, a profound embarrassment for the British in front of their American hosts. Thankfully, Marshall leaped in with a vital offer of 300 American Sherman tanks for his beleaguered ally, and Churchill was able to replace a losing team of generals with two who were to prove remarkable: Alexander as Commander-in-Chief, in Cairo, and Montgomery as the new commander of the Eighth Army in the field. Every Briton knows the outcome: the great victory over Rommel at the Battle of Alamein, a win so boosting to morale that Churchill ordered the church bells to be rung in celebration.

The African campaign was still in progress in 1943, however, and there Churchill was still able to command Roosevelt's attention in a way that not even General George C. Marshall was successful in doing.

9

THE DONKEY, THE BUFFALO AND THE BEAR

Churchill famously described the relationship between himself, Roosevelt and Stalin as like being a donkey caught between a buffalo and a bear. Characteristically Churchill added that of the three animals, only he, the donkey, knew the way . . .

As many who worked with him during the period 1942–5 went on to attest, this was a very painful time for Churchill, since he was forced, first, to realize how comparatively unimportant Britain was in the titanic struggle against Germany and Japan and, second, to see how Roosevelt would criticize him to Stalin in order to curry favour with the Soviet despot. The latter, his wartime military aide Sir Ian Jacob recalled, was especially unpleasant, and historians such as Richard Holmes have rightly commented on how regrettable this was when we look back at how the relationship between the 'Big Three' unfolded.

In many ways Churchill was fully entitled to feel hurt, and it was not very kind of Roosevelt to treat so loyal and faithful an ally in this way. In thinking he could do deals with Stalin after the war, and in hoping for post-war peace, Roosevelt might have been right, but he was hopelessly wrong and thoroughly naive in the way in which he sought to achieve it. That said, Roosevelt's decision to court Stalin at Churchill's expense was a sad but accurate reflection of changing geopolitical realities. The USSR would emerge from the Second World War as the other world superpower. Britain, despite its Empire, and despite all Churchill's fond hopes and beliefs, would simply not be in the same league.

What follows in the following three years, 1943–6, can be seen in this context, hence the very apt title of volume six of Churchill's wartime history: *Triumph and Tragedy*.

One of the reasons why the American military was despondent over being defeated over the date of D-Day is that they saw how Churchill had worked his magic over Roosevelt in setting Allied priorities in 1942. As we saw, the US Army had wanted a steady build-up – code-named *Bolero* – to be followed by the invasion of France itself, now known as *Overlord*. However, Churchill, whose devotion to the peripheral strategy was noted earlier, wanted the United States in north Africa as soon as possible, in order to bolster the sagging British campaign there. Field Marshal Auchinleck had proved no more successful than Wavell in the desert, and Rommel was still tying down British armies, and even sometimes coming very close to beating them.

The war in north Africa was not doing much harm to Hitler – the epic battles were those on the Eastern Front – but any British victory was a boost to morale, and O'Connor in 1940–1 and later on Montgomery (to become Field Marshal Viscount Montgomery of Alamein) in 1942 achieved this goal. In addition, the war in north Africa was the only place where British troops could fight the Axis *directly* and fighting them somewhere was better than sitting in fortress Britain not fighting them at all.

But the American entry into the war changed all this; now the issue was where the Americans would first engage with the enemy. Marshall, the US Army Chief of Staff, wanted to wait, but Roosevelt, a politician not a soldier, saw things from a different perspective from his generals and airmen. Churchill's winning gambit – originally code-named *Gymnast*, but known to us today as *Torch* – was simple, and it was to be his last major success.

Roosevelt wanted US troops in action *immediately* rather than allowing no combat until thirty divisions were ready to liberate Europe from Hitler. This would show the American public that the United States was already fighting the Germans in the field – we should remember that most Americans probably favoured putting the defeat of Japan over that of Hitler, since they wanted revenge for Pearl Harbor. So there was a public relations angle to Roosevelt's decision, and one that, as a politician, also helped him with Congressional elections in 1942, since, unlike Britain, the United States did not suspend the electoral process in wartime.

Marshall's option would have postponed immediate engagement, while Churchill's proposal enabled

American troops to be in combat immediately, in north Africa. So for *political* reasons, not *military*, Roosevelt sided with Churchill against his own Army Chief of Staff, Marshall. It should be added that Stalin shared Marshall's disappointment at the decision, as both men realized that if the first major United States military operation was to be in north Africa, this would completely rule out the launch of a second front against Germany in France from happening in 1943, as both the United States military and the Soviet leadership would have preferred. The tide on the Eastern Front turned to the Russian advantage during that period, especially after Stalingrad, but we know that with hindsight: it was not at all obvious at the time.

So Churchill prevailed – for the moment.

El Alamein was an enormous boost to British morale, and enabled the British to remember that they could beat the Germans. It was, though, a misleading victory, in that it was the last time that a predominantly British and Empire army beat the Axis: thereafter the major battles were to be fought alongside the Americans. And with US troops came American commanders – no longer could the British make major military decisions on their own. Churchill's days as an independent warlord were over and all operations were now firmly part of coalition warfare.

Joint force operations, despite the Soviets being on the Allied side, was predominantly US–UK in nature: there was never the same degree of integration with the Soviet high command as existed with the Anglo-American command. Paradoxically, the person who above all else enabled this to happen was Field Marshal Sir John Dill, now Head of the Joint Staff Mission in Washington who

Churchill continued to underestimate as much as the Americans esteemed him.

During this period, Churchill's tight grip on the war machine still helped him greatly. He saw the three Chiefs of Staff – Brooke (Army), Portal (RAF) and Cunningham (Navy) almost daily, and Brooke probably more frequently than that. By contrast, Roosevelt would not see the equivalents for days on end, and in addition he liked to play them against each other, especially as that enabled him to arbitrate, such as over strategy or policy disputes between Admiral King, the Chief of Naval Staff, and the US Navy, on the one hand, and Marshall and the US Army, on the other. (The US Air Force was still part of the US Army at this time).

The result was, to use a modern phrase, that while the British always got their act together and were fully coordinated, the same was not true of the United States. While Brooke frequently disagreed, often very strongly, with Churchill – for instance, vetoing the Prime Minister's desire to invade Norway again (*Jupiter*) – he would never let on in public, or in strategy discussions with the United States. But that was not the case with the Americans, with King often disagreeing volubly with his colleagues and in the open.

In January 1943 Roosevelt made one of his very rare foreign trips, to Casablanca, in Morocco, not long after the first American troops, under Eisenhower, had arrived in north Africa. All the British political and military leadership came, fully coordinated, and the Americans all at sixes and sevens. Churchill won all his major military arguments, including what to do once north Africa was liberated – which happened by May that year: the next Anglo-American target would be Sicily, from which an invasion of the Italian mainland could then be launched.

The conference had been convened in order to find out where to go next, now that British and US troops were fighting alongside each other in north Africa, the result of Churchill's campaign to postpone D-Day and to get American soldiers fighting the enemy as soon as possible. It was also important since the two Western leaders were meeting without Stalin, and so this was one of the last major occasions upon which Churchill could treat with Roosevelt as an equal.

Churchill did lose one battle – albeit temporarily – with Roosevelt, one that would have dire consequences for Britain years later, in 1963 and 1968, when the United Kingdom attempted to enter the European Economic Community. Since 1940 Churchill had given refuge to General Charles de Gaulle, the leader of the Free French and a rather awkward man who regarded himself as the embodiment of France and of resistance to Hitler. Unfortunately for both de Gaulle and Churchill, Roosevelt strongly preferred an alternative leader for France, General Giraud. The Americans insisted that de Gaulle agree to work with Giraud, and Churchill was given the unpleasant task of breaking the bad news to de Gaulle. It became very obvious to de Gaulle that Churchill was putting American wishes ahead of the Entente Cordiale, a slight de Gaulle never forgot; he insisted on seeing the United Kingdom as the lap-dog of America, and thus unworthy of joining the Europe-wide organization, now called the EU, that was to be created in the 1950s.

The Casablanca conference is also famous for Roosevelt's decision to go for 'unconditional surrender' by Germany, Italy and Japan. Churchill claimed he did not know of this in advance – this has been disputed – but decided to go along with it anyway, and in doing so he was surely right, although this was a controversial decision both then and since. The very conditional surrender of Germany in 1918 had led to the 'stab in the back' legend that the Germans could have fought on and won, a myth that Hitler was able to exploit to the full in his rise to power and afterwards. This time Germany would be defeated totally and such a legend would never again be able to rise. Germany was pulverized in 1944–5, and has been a democracy since 1949, so unlike the situation after 1918. Churchill and Roosevelt were thus right at Casablanca to insist on unconditional surrender.

July and August 1943 saw the most important battle of the war in Europe, the greatest tank battle in history, the Battle of Kursk, between the Red Army and the Germans. It is virtually unknown in the West, but Western historians such as Norman Davies and Laurence Rees are surely correct to ascribe it central importance as a major turning point. It changed the direction of the Eastern Front campaign, after which Stalin's legions never needed to look back. Victory over the Third Reich was now just a matter of time.

Also, by this time American politicians and military were working in full agreement with each other. They would no longer tolerate any delays in launching the invasion of France, and now, unlike the previous year, Roosevelt completely accepted the proposals of Marshall. *Overlord* was no longer to be postponed, though

Churchill was still trying to hold it up as late as March 1944.

Up until now – as we saw at the Casablanca conference in January 1943 – it had been just possible for Churchill to think himself as Roosevelt's equal in some way or another. In terms of troops in the field in Europe this would remain true more or less until the time of D-Day, after which American troops would predominate as overwhelmingly in Europe as their forces did in the war against Japan in Asia. However, as we also know, over 85 per cent of German troops were fighting not against the Western Allies but on the Eastern Front against the USSR. So now, as Roosevelt fully understood, and to Churchill's increasing despair, the United Kingdom was an ever less important belligerent in the struggle against the Third Reich. As former Churchill Archivist Piers Brendon has accurately described it:

> The truth was that, with the American war effort now well into its stride, Britain had become the junior partner . . . He [Churchill] could uphold Britain's status as a great power by his grand manner . . . But he had to acknowledge Britain's weakness in practice.

Roosevelt would not travel to Britain for a private pre-summit meeting to discuss the final details for the German invasion with Churchill on his own – an Anglo-American preliminary gathering – and since Stalin did not want to go too far beyond the Soviet borders – the dictator was always paranoid and hated travel – Churchill had to agree to meet where Roosevelt and Stalin wished, at the Iranian capital, Tehran.

The Tehran Conference (*Eureka*), held in the Iranian capital in late November 1943, saw Churchill truly outgunned and outnumbered, and his ability to postpone D-Day gone too: it would be in May 1944 whether he wanted it to be or not. (As we know, the actual date was 6 June 1944; so Churchill obtained a postponement, but only a small one.) Stalin and Roosevelt were in agreement as were the President with his military.

Worse news for Churchill at Tehran was the way in which Roosevelt ganged up with Stalin against him. Richard Holmes put it well:

> Much of Winston's moral authority rested on his opposition to the policy of setting a good example to dictators by unilaterally foregoing traditional means of discussion. Despite this, however, FDR convinced himself that Winston was now the fly in his soup of fellowship with the Soviet tyrant.

Roosevelt went out of his way to meet Stalin one to one, and to remind the Soviet leader on how many issues he, Roosevelt, and Churchill disagreed. He was to do the same at the meeting in Yalta, in the Crimea, the following year.

As Holmes concludes:

> The most charitable interpretation of FDR's behaviour towards Winston at Tehran and Yalta is that a policy decision was taken to establish good relations with Stalin at any cost, because without a long-term US commitment to Europe, at that time considered out of the question, the Soviet Union was certain to become the dominant regional power.

All this shows just how much western Europe owes to Truman, and to Roosevelt – but only in that he was accidentally wise enough to make Truman his Vice-President on the Democratic ticket in 1944. American troops had withdrawn from Europe in 1919, not to return to mainland Europe until D-Day in 1944. It was widely presumed at the time – certainly by Roosevelt – that the same situation would apply when Hitler had been defeated. Now we know that US troops never left – they remain in Germany to this day – and that the NATO alliance was established in 1949, all thanks to Truman.

But in 1943 US troops were earmarked either to go home after VE-Day or to fight against Japan, since before Hiroshima and Nagasaki altered the picture it was widely presumed in 1943–5 that the war against Japan would last for many years to come. To be fair to Roosevelt, the latter did weigh heavily upon him, since the presumption was that the Soviet Union, which in 1943 was strictly neutral in relation to Japan, needed coaxing to come into the war against the Japanese on the Allied side.

Either way, though, the whole Tehran experience was very humiliating for Churchill. He did not attend Roosevelt's funeral in 1945 and, though it is hard to know for sure, one wonders whether the humiliation at the President's hand played some unconscious part in Churchill's decision not to go. For Churchill, the great imperialist, the loss of British prestige was a personal blow as well as a trumpeting of Britain's now reduced global status. In public he remained steadfastly loyal to his American superiors, but in private his sorrow was clear to see, as became increasingly apparent as the climax of the struggle against Germany came nearer.

It could, though, not have been any other way. For if Churchill was frustrated at his evident powerlessness, it was the flip side of the right decision he had made back in 1940. Only with the United States could Britain hope not only to survive, but to be on the winning side, able positively to defeat Hitler, rather than just avoid the negative of defeat and conquest, as had seemed all too possible in 1940–1. So, yes, Britain's junior status was there for all to see. But the British were soon to be on the same side as the victors, the United States, the liberators of western Europe, as we shall now see.

10

D-DAY TO VICTORY

On 5 June 1944, the night before D-Day, Churchill was profoundly anxious, fearing lest, as he confided to Clementine when they had dinner alone together, 20,000 or more Allied troops might well die on the beaches of Normandy. His Chief of the Imperial General Staff, Sir Alan Brooke, shared many similar fears. As two people who had witnessed the carnage of the trenches in the First World War, their alarm was only natural. But it was also profoundly misplaced, certainly so far as the landings of the Allied troops were concerned. Only at Omaha was there anything like the major casualties that Churchill and Brooke feared, and even there, there was nowhere near the scale of the Western Front 1914–18. A new age of warfare had dawned, one that Marshall and Eisenhower understood, but which Churchill alas did not.

D-Day itself, 6 June 1944, was the most successful amphibious invasion in history, and one of the greatest feats of military logistics of all time. While it took longer to get to Caen, the first major town, than the original plans allowed, we should not forget the sheer magnitude of the Western Allies landing as many troops as they did. The weather could potentially have wreaked havoc, and caused major postponement, yet nothing was delayed more than a few hours, and the bridgehead of which the Americans had dreamed was created successfully, showing what an achievement *Overlord* represents. And now, too, Stalin could no longer make the claim that the Allies were fighting the Germans at Soviet expense, since although the British, Canadians and Americans still had fewer troops than the Red Army, they were at least in north-west Europe at last.

Not all was rosy on 6 June, however. While thousands of troops landed comparatively safely – Omaha excepted, it remains true, as Anthony Beevor and others have reminded us – real carnage was caused by Allied bombardment, including over 20,000 French civilian casualties. More non-combatant French men, women and children died in Normandy in 1944 than were killed in Britain by the Luftwaffe even during the very worst of the Blitz. Beevor is surely right to point out that the people of Normandy, and those of the *département* of Calvados in particular, paid a very high price indeed for the liberation of the rest of France, where civilian casualties were much lower, and mainly caused by the obscene massacres of whole communities by retreating SS divisions, some of the very worst atrocities of the whole war.

While Allied troops, under General Montgomery, continued the advance – defeat of the German 7th Army in the Falaise Pocket would take until August, but assault on Germany itself was delayed until 1945 – Churchill, even during the fighting in Normandy, remained passionately determined to continue fighting in the Mediterranean, and in Italy in particular (Monte Cassino had been taken by the Allies in May).

This was the famous peripheral approach we saw earlier, attacking the enemy not head-on but at outlying vulnerable points, or what Churchill called his 'soft-underbelly' approach. This shows that he was at least consistent, since this had been precisely the rationale for attacking Gallipoli in 1915: attack the Ottoman Empire rather than the main German enemy in Flanders. But, unlike during the First World War in 1915–16, Britain was now very much the junior partner in the war. Having been deprived of their desire to launch D-Day in 1943, the Americans were determined not to let Churchill get away with deflecting effort from what they perceived to be the main strategy now: attack the Third Reich directly, through north-west Europe.

Churchill also came up with the notion of an Allied attack through an area known as the Ljubljana Gap, in what is now Slovenia. Politically, it is easy to see why this latter notion was attractive: British and American forces could invade Central Europe *if* they made it through the Gap, and then press on to Vienna and thence to much of Central Europe. But unfortunately for Churchill, Allied forces in Italy were making painfully slow progress up the peninsula, and were still nowhere near the Yugoslav border in the north-east.

Furthermore, this idea was a rare one in that the British and American Chiefs of Staff united against

Churchill and declared to him with equal vigour that the notion was completely impossible, strategically and otherwise. Not only that, but Roosevelt was equally hostile to it, since he realized that the casualties in such terrain overwhelmingly favoured the defenders (as was also proving to be the case in Italy) and that Allied casualties would be massive: and all for what was essentially a *political* objective. So *Armpit* – as this mooted operation was unfortunately named – never got off the ground.

Militarily speaking, Churchill's ideas of Western troops marching victoriously into Central Europe ahead of the Soviets were alas a non-starter. In addition, in the case of Austria they proved unnecessary. Those who know the great Graham Greene thriller (and the more famous film version) *The Third Man* will know that much of Austria, including the capital, Vienna, was occupied by the Soviets. But in 1955 they retreated, leaving Austrian soil altogether, their only retreat of that kind throughout the Cold War. British and American deaths to liberate Vienna ahead of the Red Army would have been for nothing. As for Czechoslovakia, in 1945 General Patton was within miles of being able to liberate the Czech capital, Prague, himself, and only failed to do so because by then it was too late to change the agreed post-war borders and power arrangements made at Yalta that year with Stalin. Patton's troops got as far as they did without any carnage in Slovenia, which is what a Ljubljana Gap invasion would have produced.

This may seem a mere detail, but what it shows is that Churchill was no longer as important as he had been – the big players were now Stalin and Roosevelt, and with the President keen for the USSR to come in against Japan there was not much chance that Churchill's worries about growing Soviet power were going to have much traction with the White House. Plenty of Americans lower down the scale, such as George Keenan, then a US State Department official, and later a famous Cold War specialist, *did* understand Churchill's concerns fully, but they were not important enough to change anything, and, as we now know, the US Administration had in it Soviet spies such as Harry Dexter White who were doing all they could to turn American policy in the other direction, in favour of Stalin.

While it is possible to understand Churchill's wish to invade the Reich through part of Slovenia, the same sympathy cannot really extend to his zealous opposition to an Allied landing in the south of France, that had, pre-D-Day been designed to help draw German troops away from the beaches of Normandy and would now help Allied forces in northern France. This plan was originally code-named *Anvil*, but later became *Dragoon*, as Churchill felt dragooned into it by the Americans!

The idea was to remove six divisions from the Italian front and invade southern France, forcing the German armies in that country to fight on two fronts. Churchill was not happy about this, nor was General Alexander, the British Allied commander in Italy. But at Tehran Stalin had agreed with the Americans, so there was nothing that Churchill could now do but complain. He delayed as long as he could, but by August 1944 it was too late to stop it, and the Americans were able to land near Marseilles almost unopposed.

Historians differ on how effective *Dragoon* turned out to be. For Richard Holmes, for instance, the impact on the main battles were negligible, but for others the need for the Germans to deal with the Allied thrust from the south, and the need for the Germans to send troops to combat them, helped to make all the difference to the speed with which the Americans in northern Europe were able to extricate themselves from the Battle of the Bulge after Hitler's surprise last great offensive of the war, in the Ardennes at the end of 1944. By now it is probably hard to know who is right, and how much difference was made to the war by the movement of divisions from Italy to France. The main thing is that Churchill felt deeply his growing lack of importance in American perception compared to the ever-increasing stature of Stalin, despite the overwhelming evidence of the sheer brutality of the Soviet regime. Additionally, this is the background to one of the most extraordinary episodes of the war in which Churchill was involved – his trip to Moscow to see Stalin in the autumn of 1944, to create what has become known as the 'Percentages Agreement'.

In essence, what Churchill and Stalin did was to carve up zones of influence between them, partitioning Central and Eastern Europe in a similar fashion to the Great Powers after the defeat of Napoleon in 1815. The Red Army was now poised to recapture huge swathes of the region, and Churchill wanted to be sure that he could have some influence on the post-war map of Europe. Some countries, such as Romania and Bulgaria, were deemed by the two men to be in the Soviet sphere of influence – 75 per cent to 90 per cent under Soviet control – while Greece, for instance, about which Churchill felt deeply, would be firmly in the Western/British zone. More interesting was the fate of Hungary and Yugoslavia. In the original discussion both were to be 50 per cent British, 50 per cent Soviet, but at a subsidiary meeting of the Foreign Ministers – Eden and Molotov – the latter was able to bully Eden into conceding the lion's share of Hungary to the USSR. Only Yugoslavia was to remain equally shared.

The sheer cynicism, not to say immorality, of this is quite breathtaking! Churchill always referred to it as his 'naughty document' and it is easy to see why. He was carving up the fate of millions of innocent peoples, of Bulgarians, Yugoslavs, Greeks and Romanians, with one of the worst dictators in history, and with no reference to those who actually lived in the countries whatsoever. It is not surprising that the Americans were outraged – as one of them joked, how could you split countries that way: could someone be only 70 per cent pregnant? Their criticism is, entirely justified, in that the agreement also enabled Stalin to say that he had a Western imprimatur to conquer for the USSR a whole region of Europe, and to impose communist governments upon the poor countries in question after the war.

However, while the American view is indeed valid, the fact is that *Stalin actually kept his side of the bargain after 1945*...

This is what makes the 'Percentages Agreement', drawn up so casually, such an extraordinary document. Greece, despite the large communist resistance movement that wished to take that country over in the same way that Tito prevailed in Yugoslavia, remained firmly in the Western camp, with Churchill himself visiting the country and using British troops to re-impose the monarchy and a regime favourable to Britain. The communists got no assistance at all from Stalin. Not only that, but Stalin did nothing to prevent Tito from breaking away from the Soviet bloc in 1948, while suppressing ruthlessly and often bloodily similar attempts in Poland and Hungary in the 1950s, and Czechoslovakia in 1968.

Yugoslavia was the one remaining 50/50 country of the Stalin–Churchill deal, and from 1948 onwards it was a communist country, but one that was neutral in the Cold War. It was also the one People's Republic that allowed its citizens to travel freely outside its borders, with millions doing so, especially as guest workers in Germany. As one Yugoslav once put it, the country was still a cage – no pluralist liberal democracy there – but it was very much a 'big cage' in comparison with the Soviet bloc countries under Moscow's rule.

The 'Percentages Agreement' extorted a terrible price, if you were Bulgarian, Romanian or Hungarian – Churchill had, in effect, given up on your freedom and for all intents and purposes handed you over to Stalin. From 1944–89 these countries, plus Poland, Czechoslovakia and the DDR (East Germany) were firmly under the Soviet yoke.

On Poland, Churchill cared deeply, and the fate of that unhappy country, squeezed geographically between Germany and the USSR, was, to him, a very integral part of the 'tragedy' of the *Triumph and Tragedy* of his final volume of history of the war. He was right: Britain had gone to war to save Poland in 1939, and instead of genuine freedom the Poles had ended up simply acquiring one foreign tyranny in place of another. It is significant that the Poles whom Laurence Rees interviewed for his book and television documentary on the Allies and Stalin were all so deeply critical of and hostile to Churchill, a man whom they regarded as having betrayed them at the end of the war. They had fought bravely alongside British troops in campaigns such as the Battle of Britain, and at Monte Cassino in Italy and Arnhem in the Netherlands, but all to no avail as Poland passed from Nazi hands into those of the Soviets.

While Churchill was very strict with the Free Poles, whose base was in London (until 1990, when Lech Walesa became President of the Republic of Poland), in private he did all he could to intercede with Roosevelt to take a much tougher line with Stalin over the vexed issue of genuine free elections in Poland after the war, something that the Soviet dictator, needless to add, was more than reluctant to allow. But, as many American diplomats who did not share their President's continued lack of understanding towards the British leader noted, Churchill was not in a strong moral position when it came to Poland, since he had already sold the Hungarians, Romanians and Bulgarians down the river to Stalin in 1944 in his 'Percentages Agreement', as both the Soviet dictator and Roosevelt knew. It is hard to be trusted as having real concern about the freedom of one country when you have shown complete lack of concern for the freedom of three others.

By the end of 1944 Roosevelt was becoming physically weaker, and he died in April 1945, just before the war in Europe ended. His overwhelming concern was to win the war, do a deal with Stalin that would also help the new United Nations organization that the President was creating, and get the troops home from Europe to beat Japan, in the latter case with the expectation of Soviet aid. While it is the case that many in the US Administration were as worried about the fate of Poland as Churchill, there was nothing that could be done to override Roosevelt's wish to reach some sort of rapprochement with Stalin.

This was enshrined at the last ever meeting of the 'Big Three', in February 1945, in the Crimean resort town of Yalta, a place that has now become infamous, associated in the minds of many (including many Conservative MPs at the time, who voted against Churchill on the results of the conference) with a new kind of appeasement, in this case of the USSR instead of Hitler and the Third Reich.

Churchill came to Yalta with a real sense of despair. He wanted to reassemble the pre-war world, and now saw that this was to be utterly impossible: the 'new and nasty' world, to use Richard Holmes's phrase, was the only show on offer.

The problem was that to Stalin possession was the law, and, unlike the Western Allies, he had troops in Poland and they did not. As the tragedy of the Warsaw Uprising in September 1944 shows, the Soviet attitude to Polish freedom differed precious little from that of the Nazis, with their armies deciding to wait outside the Polish capital, delaying the fight against the Third Reich, until the Nazis had been able to finish off the brave Warsaw rebels. Churchill's wishes to help the courageous leaders of the Warsaw Uprising were quashed by Stalin, who was as keen to see the deaths of independent-minded freedom-loving Poles as much as Hitler and the SS. Not until the rebellion was completely crushed by the Germans did Soviet armies recommence the attack, and countless Polish resistance fighters and patriots who had survived the Nazis were then brutally put to death by the supposedly liberating Russian forces.

How could the West have helped? Some authors, John Grigg among them, have argued that a D-Day in 1943 would have enabled the Western Allies to meet the Soviets on the Vistula and not the Elbe, and had that indeed been the case, Poland could have been the free country its millions of inhabitants wished it to be. Other historians, such as Sir Max Hastings, Carlo D'Este and Andrew Roberts, disagree strongly that an earlier Western invasion would have worked. And the truth is that since *Overlord* – the second front – began in June 1944, it is alas very hard indeed to see what on earth the United Kingdom and the United States could have done to help the Poles effectively and prevent what was in fact a repressive Russian occupation for over forty years. The Soviets were in occupation, the Allied troops many miles away and thus in no possible position to alter the outcome.

Churchill was also alarmed at the Soviet seizure of so much Polish and East German territory by the USSR (some of which, in former German East Prussia, in Kaliningrad, remains part of Russia to this day). Much time was spent in 1943–5 on the Polish-Soviet and Polish-German border questions, all of which were resolved in favour of Stalin's wishes. Though this was tragic for millions of people, many of whom died in terrible ethnic cleansing (as we now call it) after 1945, as borders shifted by sometimes hundreds of miles, there was again nothing much that Roosevelt or Churchill could have done to ensure a different result. Once again, Soviet troops were in firm military possession, and it would have taken a third world war (a possibility that Churchill did contemplate, at least in theory) to dislodge them.

So that is why historians such as Norman Davies are right to say that so far as the war against Hitler was concerned, the *real* victors were the Soviets, not the British or Americans. Stalin was able to establish a vast cordon sanitaire around the USSR, the countries within it soon becoming known either as the Soviet bloc or, misleadingly in geographic terms, as 'Eastern Europe'. The Cold War, which many date to events such as the Berlin Airlift of 1948–9 or to the Communist seizure of power in Prague in 1948, can more properly be said to have its origins in who conquered what in the last year of the war.

(It is very important indeed to add here that such a comment is not in any way to belittle the heroic sacrifice of thousands of immensely brave and courageous Western forces in the liberation of their part of Europe in 1944–5. Far from it. But remember, and it is worth repeating: around 300,000 Western deaths in the war, and over *twenty million* Soviets, not to forget the fact that *85 per cent* of German forces fought on the *Eastern* and not the *Western* Front, as Stalin well knew.)

Perhaps the tragedy of all this is that in the earlier part of the war, when he could have made more difference, Churchill, like Roosevelt, was concentrating wholly on wining the conflict, and not thinking at all of what would happen after the war was over. This was often to the despair of Anthony Eden, for whom such planning was vital, not least in order to secure post-war British influence. By the time that Churchill actually realized what was happening, in a way that Roosevelt failed to do, it was far too late, since the Red Army was already in occupation of vast swathes of Central and Eastern Europe.

So if it was already too late by Tehran in late 1943, for Churchill to have a say in the new post-war order, by early 1945, and the Yalta Conference held on Soviet soil, it was well past being far too, and overwhelmingly, late. Soviet boots on the ground, and Stalin's acute grasp of geopolitical possibilities, had won the day. So, at Yalta, the impotent remonstrations of Churchill came to nothing and Stalin forced a communist government on Poland. In addition, the final prong of attack on Germany was debated as well as its future once conquest had been achieved.

We now need to take a diversion from international affairs and turn to the Home Front, and how Churchill dealt with matters that had no bearing on the war itself, but were of huge interest to the British electorate, who had suffered greatly in the Depression years before 1939.

One of the criticisms of Churchill in his later years is that he ignored domestic affairs at the expense of foreign and military matters. In one sense, this does not matter: the war was rightly his priority and his overwhelming focus of attention. Yet much of significance was achieved during the period.

In 1944 the Education Act completely changed British schooling, with a dramatic improvement in secondary education that for over thirty years (depending upon your politics; others would say 'ever since') enabled clever children from poorer homes to receive the kind of education that had been completely out of reach for most of them hitherto. Generations of working-class pupils were able to have not only a wonderful secondary school education, but also to get into university, and more than just to Oxford or Cambridge. Social mobility was transformed overnight, and for the next half-century was to be hugely better than it had ever been before.

In addition, the Beveridge Report of 1942, by Sir William (later Lord) Beveridge created the consensus that was soon to lead, in the post-war Labour Government of 1945–51, to the establishment of the National Health Service (NHS), enabling even the poorest to have free access to the very best healthcare, and an institution that in the twenty-first century remains, now at infinitely greater financial cost, very much in place. Significantly, when Churchill was in power in 1951–5 he left the NHS firmly unchanged, and while Conservatives (notably Margaret Thatcher) have tinkered with the way in which the NHS is run, all the major political parties have kept zealously to the sacrosanct policy of keeping the NHS going.

Both these reforms originated under Churchill as Coalition Prime Minister 1940–5, with Labour and Liberal as well as Conservatives in the government. Purist Tories might have objected, but they were often the same people who had distrusted Churchill and supported Neville Chamberlain before the war. While he was to resume partisan politics with a vengeance after May 1945, Churchill effectively devolved domestic politics often to those not sharing his views during the conflict, with results in both education and health that were to live long after him.

Many Parliamentary by-elections were held during the Second World War when MPs either died of old age or were killed in action, since many chose to fight rather than to be full-time politicians at Westminster (the same choice that we saw Churchill himself make during his brief time on the Western Front in 1916). When war began there was a pact between the principal parties not to contest seats held by others, which in effect froze the balance of power in the House of Commons to what it had been in September 1939 – a massive Conservative-National Government majority, with a few Labour gains at by-elections 1935–9.

However, by 1942–3 ordinary people were increasingly deciding at by-elections to vote against the Conservatives and their much smaller National Liberal and National Labour allies. Such candidates could not be officially from the Labour Party, and, during the war, a briefly existing left-wing party called Common Wealth arose, winning several key by-elections to Parliament, right down to 1945. This was not necessarily against Churchill as war leader, but it was most certainly against the Conservative Party, of which he had been leader since Chamberlain's death in 1940.

On 12 April 1945 Roosevelt died, to be succeeded by his Vice-President, Harry Truman, who only then found out about the research undertaken to produce atomic bombs. Then, on 30 April 1945, Hitler committed suicide in his bunker in Berlin, with Soviet troops by this stage on his doorstep.

The fall of Berlin to Soviet forces swiftly followed, and surrender in the West to British forces led by Field Marshal Montgomery. The war in Europe was over: Germany surrendered – unconditionally as per the Casablanca agreement – on 8 May 1945. Millions of people rejoiced – the most terrible conflict in the history of Europe was now finished, and victory had come at last. VE-Day – victory in Europe – was celebrated wildly all over the United Kingdom. Not only was Britain safe but the Nazis had been defeated conclusively and overwhelmingly, without any of the ambiguity of the German surrender back in 1918. Churchill was cheered to the rafters when he appeared with the royal family on the balcony of Buckingham Palace, as the man who had led his country through the very worst, and brought the fight to the most glorious conclusion.

But, of course, the Second World War was not actually over. Japan was on the way down, but had not been finally defeated. With the effect of the atomic bombs soon to be dropped on Japan still unknown, it was widely thought that the war against the Japanese could last well into 1946 or even beyond. *Final* victory over all the nation's foes was thus thought to be possibly some way into the future, even if Britain's closest enemy, the Third Reich, was now a smouldering ruin.

Churchill's idea was to continue the wartime Government coalition until the end of *all* hostilities, which in practice meant the defeat of Japan. Priority had been given by the United States to the conquest of Germany, but America's focus now shifted to what it thought was going to be the long-haul conquest of the rest of the Pacific, and then the Japanese themselves.

However, when VE-Day came the Labour Party decided that with the country's nearest enemy, Germany, vanquished, it was time to resume normal politics. So in May 1945 the great and now victorious wartime coalition ended, with the Labour and Liberal parties returning to their pre-1940 opposition status. It was also decided that as Parliament had been artificially prolonged because of the war (five years being the maximum allowed under normal circumstances) and there had been no general election since 1935, now ten years before, one should be called as soon as possible. Parliament was thus dissolved, and since millions of soldiers, sailors and airmen, all of whom had the vote in their home constituencies, were spread throughout the world, it was agreed that the result would be deferred until July to allow time for all the votes to be gathered in and counted.

In the meantime, Churchill became interim Prime Minister, presiding over what was basically a Conservative administration, with a few National Liberal allies, as had been the case prior to 1940.

Clementine, who was still really a Liberal at heart, thought this a huge mistake. She did not like the idea of her exhausted husband, who was now over seventy years of age, becoming a partisan politician again, and she would far rather that he had retired. This would have guaranteed his reputation, since he could then have gone out on the news of victory, the hero and saviour of his nation, and his pre-war partisan reputation would have been forgotten.

However, Churchill loved politics, both for what he felt he could still achieve, and also, many biographers and psychologists have argued – surely with much merit

– because the continued activity of high office was the perfect antidote to his otherwise crippling 'Black Dog' depression, which had afflicted him since childhood, and which, his physician Lord Moran's diaries confirm, remained with him as powerful and malign as ever. Either way (and probably for both reasons) he decided to ignore Clementine's advice and persist, now as a Conservative Prime Minister in an election battle against those in the Labour Party who had been his colleagues for the five years of wartime partnership.

The election campaign was fought without the benefit of the extensive opinion polling that we take for granted today – though it would have been hard to poll the millions of soldiers spread around the globe, from Germany to Burma, the latter still very much at war with the Japanese. As a result, Churchill presumed that he would win, much as Lloyd George had won the 'Khaki Election' in similar circumstances back in 1918. After all, he had saved Britain from the Nazis, and surely the electorate would reward him accordingly?

In fact, this proved to be a complete delusion. On the one hand, the ecstatic and very genuine cheer that greeted Churchill when he appeared on the balcony of Buckingham Palace on VE-Day showed that the British people were indeed profoundly grateful to him *as war leader* and, as the historian A.J.P. Taylor has rightly called him, the 'saviour of his country'. Everyone agreed on that, regardless of their political preferences, since it was indisputably true. On the other hand, he was no longer the leader of the all-party winning war coalition, in which politicians had put partisan differences aside in the country's hours of need. He was now standing as *leader of the Conservative Party*, and that is how the electors now saw him.

There is a sad irony in all this, from Churchill's point of view. Throughout the 1930s the Conservative-dominated National Government had kept him resolutely out of office, and, as we saw, not just over appeasement, where he was right, but over other issues such as India and his support of Edward VIII as well. As a result, Churchill had indeed been a Conservative MP during this period, but, excluded from power, he had not been responsible for any of the Government's actions, domestic or foreign. *But he was now Conservative leader.* The one thing that most British people were determined upon was that they never wanted to go back to the mass unemployment and poverty of the 1930s ever again. Churchill's genius had won the war, but the British people were now voting on domestic issues *not* upon his conduct as wartime Prime Minister. So Churchill, as leader of his party, was being judged on the conduct of that party when in government in the 1930s – even though he had spent those 'Wilderness Years' entirely on the backbenches.

Churchill did not understand this, and nor, it should be added, did millions around the world, including those in the United States, who only knew the wartime hero, and who had no knowledge of the internal domestic politics of Britain pre-1939, other than that Neville Chamberlain and his policy of appeasement had let the country down badly.

Churchill's handling of the campaign itself was highly controversial, especially the speech he made implying that the Labour Party, if elected, would introduce so many state controls that it would have to create something akin to a Gestapo – the dreaded Nazi secret police – to make sure people obeyed them. To make such a draconian accusation against people who had so recently been his colleagues in the fight against Nazism was distinctly unwise, and proved to be unhelpful to the Conservative Party. Called 'one of the worst-judged acts of Churchill's political career . . .', which was now nearly half a century old, it also brought back to voters' minds Churchill's pre-1940 reputation for intemperate language and political unreliability. As John Keegan observes, 'he was seen by the man and woman in the street as a reactionary. His reputation was anti-worker and anti-welfare.' Since the Labour Party was now advocating the creation of a massive welfare state, of the kind for which Beveridge had argued, Churchill was now profoundly out of step with the times.

But even in early July defeat for Churchill was still widely regarded as unthinkable. That month he went off to Potsdam, for the first post-war conference of major leaders, held in a palace on the outskirts of Berlin, the now conquered German capital. Held to discuss the war in the Pacific and the final moves against the Japanese, this would be Churchill's first meeting with Harry Truman, the new American President. The Leader of the Opposition Clement Attlee was also there, though not expecting that he would soon be Prime Minister.

Yet when the results were announced, on 26 July, it was to declare a massive landslide victory for the Labour Party, its first ever majority government (the two previous times in power had been with Liberal support). To the astonishment of Stalin, for whom genuine democracy was a complete mystery, it was now Attlee who returned to sign the Potsdam Declaration (calling for Japanese surrender; in fact, it would be mid-August, after the bombing of Hiroshima and Nagasaki, before the Allies could celebrate VJ-Day) as Prime Minister, as Churchill had been hurled from office. The British people had spoken decisively, and in favour of one of the most radical governments ever to hold power in British history. Churchill's five years of power were over.

11

THE ELDER STATESMAN

When Churchill went down to heavy defeat in the 1945 general election, Clementine tried to cheer him up by saying that it might well be a blessing in disguise, to which he famously retorted that if that was the case, then the blessing was very deeply disguised. So the saviour of his nation left Downing Street not in triumph, as his wartime achievements would have suggested, but in ignominious political defeat, at the hands of those who had been, throughout the war, his allies in the struggle against Hitler. In the days before opinion polls, no one, including Churchill himself – perhaps *especially* the great man himself – could have ever anticipated so strange an ending to his tenure of wartime power and victory.

It might have been better for his reputation if he had retired then and there, as his wife had wanted him to do, because his glory days were well and truly over. He was to lead his party for another decade and to be Prime

Minister again from 1951–5, a time that has been referred to as his 'Indian summer'.

Much of his time as Leader of the Opposition was spent in writing his wartime memoirs, disguised as an objective history of the Second World War. Needless to say, all six volumes became massive international best-sellers, and they helped Churchill both financially (he was given a publisher's advance of £600,000: sixty times his salary as Prime Minister!) and in terms of building up support for his position having been the only right one to hold. He had said that history would look on him favourably because he would write the history, and these six volumes certainly fulfilled the role that he intended for them. For Churchill is indisputably the hero of his own work, the man who knew, and this created the legend that we know so well today.

However, there is one major problem: now that the archives on Churchill's epic work *The Second World War* are available to us, we can see how Churchill rewrote history in order to put himself in a good light in considering his actions during the war. In his book *In Command of History*, British historian David Reynolds has shown beyond doubt that Churchill strongly manipulated the facts to fit the picture he wanted us to have, rather than give a full and unvarnished picture of what actually happened and why. At that time British government documents were secret in perpetuity – it was only some while later that one could see non-intelligence related files thirty years old and more – so Churchill would have assumed that what he wrote in his books would never be checked up on by historians able to see the actual files themselves.

Moreover, Churchill really had no right to keep such a vast treasure trove of Top Secret Government papers in his own possession! But because of who he was, the Labour Government of Clement Attlee gave him special dispensation, on a scale that no other Prime Minister has enjoyed since. (There was a huge controversy decades later when the National Lottery paid millions to the Churchill family to buy these papers, so that ready access could be given to historians to examine them. This was because, in effect, the nation was buying from Churchill's heirs papers that had belonged to the British Government in the first place. Now all these papers are available at the Churchill Archives Centre in Cambridge.)

In a way the dissembling does not matter, since Churchill had rescued the British people in 1940, and had made sure that Britain was on the winning side in 1945. The *basic* thrust of the story is therefore true, and that is usually what most people remember. However, in countless details Reynolds shows that things were not *exactly* as Churchill portrayed them. This is of course the case with autobiographical writing, though Churchill portrayed his books as history, not strict autobiography, whether political or not – authors always and naturally want to portray themselves in the best possible light and even Churchill was no exception.

But these books are offered as history, and there is also the major problem in that Churchill was writing the series while still in office, as Leader of the Opposition 1945–51 and then as Prime Minister 1951–5. Most of those in public office write their accounts or memoirs after retirement, which means that they can be far more explicit about what they did, what they thought, and above all what they felt about other people. Churchill, in composing his six-volume *magnum opus* while still very much an active player, held back from being as candid as he might have liked about some of the leading players, since, as a world statesman and a practising politician he was still dealing with and soliciting favours from people as varied as Eisenhower, President of the United States from 1953, and Stalin, Soviet dictator until his death that same year. Churchill, in other words, had to pull his punches, and this makes the work not quite as informative, or completely full and accurate, as it could have been.

The books were also written by a team, of which Churchill was the chief, which consisted of several of the colleagues with whom he had worked during the war such as Sir Henry Pownall, younger researchers such as William Deakin, and plenty of wise advice from stalwarts such as General Ismay. Large swathes of the books consist of memoranda by Churchill, which rather confirmed the suspicion during the war of his colleagues that much of what he was writing during that period were not so much communications to their recipients but notes for future historical use. Seldom do we get the replies, so inevitably what we see is thus rather imbalanced. On the other hand, it should be said that readers were able to see the thoughts of the great wartime leader himself, many years before such documents were ever able to be seen by anyone else, let alone by professional historians.

The six volumes, along with Churchill's towering oratory, helped to gain him a Nobel Prize for Literature, one of the very rare non-fiction authors ever awarded that great accolade. Since for the books he was more editor-in-chief than actual author the award might thus be slightly unfair, although plenty of examples exist in the science Nobel prizes of the laureateship going to the head of a laboratory rather than to all the research team working on a particular project. And one can also say that, looking at his *entire* literary career, his achievement is unique and astonishing, and that his oratory helped, as we saw, to save Britain from Nazism in 1940–1. So perhaps the prize was rightly deserved after all.

In his Opposition years, Churchill still did not greatly involve himself in domestic politics, which he tended to leave to others, most notably to R.A. 'Rab' Butler, head of the Conservative Research Department and his Chancellor of the Exchequer after 1951. But on the international stage, he really did embody the cliché of striding the world like a colossus, since, with Roosevelt's death at the end of the war in 1945 there was simply no one else of Churchill's stature anywhere, except perhaps Stalin, who as the Soviet dictator could thus be said to be in a different category.

Two of Churchill's great themes in this period stand out above all others, one not contentious because he was so obviously right, the other still enmeshed in twenty-first century domestic political controversy.

Let us start with his legendary speech in 1946 in Fulton, Missouri, the home state of the new United States President, Harry Truman (and commemorated to this day by the Winston Churchill Memorial and Library at Westminster College in Fulton). The words in the speech that we all remember are, 'From Stettin in the

Baltic to Trieste in the Adriatic, an iron curtain has descended across the Continent . . .'.

This was now alas entirely true, and Churchill was completely right to point out the new division of Europe that Stalin had inflicted upon the poor peoples of Central and Eastern Europe in imposing communism upon them. Strictly speaking, not all of those countries were *actually* communist in 1946 – that was to come to pass over the next two years, culminating in the tragic communist coup in Czechoslovakia in 1948, when the one great beacon of democracy and civilized values and freedoms between the wars in Central Europe was snuffed out, and the millions of inhabitants of that region compelled to live under alien communist rule as subjects of Moscow for the next forty years and more, until they finally regained their freedom in 1989.

However, Churchill in 1946 was prophetically accurate, and was most certainly right *in principle* – the Soviets had 'liberated' these countries during the war, and were never going to let go their grip upon them. Europe was divided, and soon a very real iron curtain was a terrible reality as well as a metaphor for what Stalin had done.

Yet, in a not so remembered part of the speech, Churchill also stated that he hoped that the solidarity of the English-speaking peoples – in effect, Britain, the United States and the white Dominions of the Commonwealth – in combination with the United Nations, would be the answer to the new division and the new tyranny dominating Europe to its east. In this he was to be wrong.

But, three years later, Britain, Canada and the United States were at the heart of an organization that did indeed keep the peace: NATO, founded in 1949, after the shock both of the Berlin Airlift in 1948–9, when the Western Allies flew in supplies to the Soviet-besieged western sectors of Berlin, and of the tragic Prague coup of 1948. NATO, its first General Secretary, Churchill's former aide Lord Ismay, once said, was to keep the Americans in, the Russians out and the Germans down, and in all three it succeeded more than admirably.

The Cold War ended in 1989–91 not with destruction on the scale so feared by the generations forced to live in its shadow, but with freedom for the oppressed peoples not just of Central Europe, such as Poland and Czechoslovakia, but also for those states extinguished in 1940 by the Soviets, such as the Baltic Republics. All of these countries are now part of both NATO and the European Union (EU), and never again should a German or Russian invasion destroy their independence and liberty. Churchill's hope for a means of resistance to what had seemed so inevitable and uncontestable in the Second World War was thus fulfilled, some quarter-century after his death.

NATO, in one sense therefore, while created during the time when Churchill was in Opposition, can be seen nonetheless as the outcome of the kind of speeches he was making about the need to deal with the Soviet threat. The EU, or 'Europe' as it is inevitably called (mixing continent with institution), is another, but not one that Churchill ever intended for his own country, and this is where his views remain a source of acrimony and debate in Britain down to the present.

As Leader of the Opposition Churchill made a series of speeches, including a major one in Zurich in 1946, calling for the free nations of Europe to come together as a 'United States of Europe'. (The same speech also tallies with his memoirs, in that he insisted that there should be magnanimity to the war's losers, most notably Germany, and also Franco-German reconciliation after decades of mutual enmity.)

This shocked more than a few people at the time. There were those in his own party, such as Harold Macmillan and Edward Heath (each a future leader and Prime Minister), and Churchill's son-in-law Duncan Sandys, who believed strongly in Europe coming together, in a way that we would now recognize as the precursors of today's European Union. A younger generation in the Labour Party, such as future statesman Roy Jenkins, also held such beliefs, as did many of no fixed political abode.

Many young *pro*-European conservatives hoped that Churchill would lead Britain into the new European Promised Land that was now emerging on the continent. These included many who had been profoundly inspired by Churchill's Zurich speech, and those who had worked together over the Marshall Plan, which had involved much inter-Europe collaboration over its implementation. Most notable of these was the young Frenchman Jean Monnet, who was a Marshall Plan civil servant and was to be the first President of the European Economic Community Commission when that body finally came into being some years later.

However, Churchill was gravely to disappoint all such dreams, whether tragically or just as well depending upon your viewpoint of the twenty-first century EU and all it stands for. For all that he agreed to was the Council of Europe, essentially a cultural talking-shop, a body that still exists but without any real power.

NATO involved much pooling of sovereignty and much *supranational* co-operation. British and French troops, for example, had to be under the command of an American, since the Supreme Allied Commander Europe, from Eisenhower onwards, has always been a United States citizen. (France opted out of this for some while later on, only to rejoin.) But both for Churchill, and for the Labour Government of 1950–1(who felt that the trade unions would not like getting too closely involved with their European equivalents) *supranational* anything else was entirely out of the question. For Churchill it was fine if folk on the continent of Europe got together – Franco-German reconciliation being one good example – but, as he put it, he did not see Britain stooping down to the level of a country such as Belgium.

So when six European countries, including the former Axis nations of Italy and Germany, along with France and the three Benelux nations (Belgium, Netherlands and Luxembourg) pooled both their economic resources and their national sovereignty in 1950–1 to form the European Coal and Steel Community, the progenitor of today's EU, Britain stood aside and remained apart. NATO was one thing – it also included the United States and Canada – but this was another.

As Sir Roy Denman, a British and then EU diplomat, has said, Britain missed the bus, and continued to do so until the Europhile Conservative Prime Minister Edward Heath finally negotiated British entry in 1973, some four years after the death of the unremittingly anti-British General de Gaulle, who as President of France 1958–69 did all he could to keep the British out.

Denman, the *Guardian* commentator Hugo Young and others are right to say that had Britain joined the infant EEC at its creation in 1957, that institution would have been radically different from the EU we know today. Britain would have been one of the leaders from the beginning – it would not have spent its first three decades under an effective Franco-German hegemony – and would have benefited enormously from free access to the European market that all the six member states enjoyed from 1957 to 1973.

Up until this part of Churchill's life it has been possible to be as studiously politically neutral as possible. In Britain, however, the European Union, and British membership of it, has been one of the most contentious issues in domestic politics for over fifty years and it remains as divisive a topic in the twenty-first century as it was in the second half of the twentieth.

Therefore, the decisions of the second term Labour Government in 1950–1 and of the Conservative Governments of Churchill and Eden in 1951–7 *not* to join the nascent EU – the European Coal and Steel Community under Labour and the EEC under the Conservatives, remain deeply controversial. Anti-Europeans ('Eurosceptics') regard the decision to stay out as an act of wise statesmanship and patriotism, while pro-Europeans ('Europhiles') see it as a major catastrophe that has had long-term disastrous effects on the British economy ever since.

The other bone of contention is Britain's ties with the United States – what is even today called the 'Special Relationship', the continued existence of which Hillary

Clinton, as Secretary of State, felt the need to reassure the British of soon after she took office. To many Britons, links with the United States, thousands of miles away, remains a far more important bond than that with continental Europe, now a short train-ride away by Eurostar (with Paris and Brussels being closer in time and distance from London than many towns in the north of England or anywhere in Scotland). In the 2009 European Parliament elections, the UK Independence Party, which would remove Britain from the EU, did not hesitate to use a picture of Winston Churchill in their main political advertising. Few people have quoted 'Winston' more than Margaret Thatcher, the most strongly Eurosceptic Prime Minister that Britain has had – and opinion polls show that millions of British people agree with her.

From Churchill to Tony Blair, British Prime Ministers have always aimed to be as close to the United States as possible, as well as, with the exception of Margaret Thatcher, seeking close cooperation with fellow members of the EU, since British accession to the original EEC in 1973.

But, as others have said, while Britain is an equal to France and Germany, the other two major European nations, the United Kingdom is a minnow in comparison to the vast size and power of the United States. It may be a 'Special Relationship' of what Churchill fondly described as the 'English Speaking Peoples', but there is no way in which it is even remotely a relationship of equals. As indeed France and Britain were to find in 1956 when President Eisenhower pulled the plug on the Franco-British-Israeli invasion of Egypt at Suez.

What is interesting is that in recent lives of Churchill, this is an issue upon which both revisionists, such as John Charmley (in his *Churchill's Grand Alliance*), and strong advocates, such as Geoffrey Best (in his *Churchill: A Study in Greatness*), seem to agree with one another, since both of them belong to the 'missed the bus' school of thought that recognizes that Churchill's aim to create what political pundits now prefer to call the 'Anglosphere' was doomed to fail, since, as he was occasionally compelled to admit, the United States was both far more powerful and also, not surprisingly, bound to put its own national interests first rather than kow-tow to its far weaker British ally. Churchill, in other words, aimed for the best, but left office in 1955 unable to achieve those goals which he had postponed retirement to achieve.

From 1945 to 1955, when he finally retired as Prime Minister, Churchill had, however, had the moral leadership of Europe for the asking, since no one came even near his deserved and unique status. Any new Europe could have been fashioned in whatever likeness he wanted and, one should not forget, this would have been *before* de Gaulle came to power in 1958, with all the anti-British, anti-American baggage that he brought with him.

Yet, depending on one's viewpoint, Churchill either threw this away, chucking the crown in the gutter as it were, or rightly kept Britain away from something foreign and, above all, French – which is why, over sixty years after his Zurich speech, what he did resonates in the politics of the twenty-first century. Instead of a purely or solely European model, Churchill saw Britain in a unique role, somehow above the common fray, and, above all, in a 'Special Relationship' with the United States. He saw his country as part of three circles: the Anglo-American circle, the Empire-Commonwealth circle and then, finally, the European circle.

This was a view that was already archaic at the time, since the Empire was not to last in such a form for much longer. India had finally been granted its long overdue independence by the Labour Government in 1947, and the Asian nations were already nearing freedom: Sri Lanka (Ceylon) in 1948 and Malaysia in 1957, with the first African country, Ghana (Gold Coast), that year also. By the time of Churchill's death hardly anywhere was directly ruled from London any more. The Commonwealth remains a place of much emotional attachment for many – especially for the Queen – but in terms of actual importance it now counts for very little indeed, with the old white Dominions such as Canada and Australia closer, if anything, to the United States than to Britain.

Likewise, as the still controversial British decision to back the United States over Iraq in 2003 shows, the 'Special Relationship' can have its perils as well as its advantages. Not only that, but with France and Germany so much more powerful than Britain, those two countries are surely more important *politically* to the United States than the United Kingdom, although ties of culture, common language and nostalgic affection naturally remain very emotionally powerful. But with the Cold War thankfully over, the days when Britain was able, as one Foreign Secretary once said, to 'punch above its weight' are arguably long gone, and Britons visiting Washington DC soon find out how little influence

Britain actually has when it comes to decision-making and policy options in the American capital.

So that leaves the European circle, the one that the leaders of Europe pre-de Gaulle in 1958 would have dearly loved the British to join, and thus to have had the opportunity of helping shape the new post-war European landscape, but which proved impossible due to the United Kingdom's late accession in 1973. For, while Churchill had talked the talk in opposition, he certainly did not walk the walk when in power after 1951. In this he was the despair of Harold Macmillan, who could see how the future European landscape would evolve, but very much in step with the Conservative Party and in particular with the views of his long-suffering heir apparent and Foreign Secretary Anthony Eden, who fully shared Churchill's coolness to European integration at the grass roots.

Churchill narrowly lost the 1950 general election, held by statute five years after the previous one, but the fact that he came so near is extraordinary in itself, since the Labour majority in 1945 had been enormous. Then the Labour Government imploded, with the kind of internal divisions that were to plague the party for the next four decades and more. So in 1951 there was a second general election, which the Conservatives won, albeit with a small majority. Churchill was once again Prime Minister and was to hang on in office until 1955.

As before, he essentially left domestic affairs to others – 'Rab' Butler was named as Chancellor of the Exchequer, and Macmillan was a spectacularly successful Minister of Housing. Sir Walter Monckton – Edward VIII's old lawyer – became Minister of Labour, looking after the trade unions. Meanwhile, Churchill concentrated on foreign affairs, to the sorrow of Eden, whose supposed bailiwick they were.

Churchill was fully aware of the dangerous situation in which western Europe now found itself. The Iron Curtain was never far away, the symbol of a divided continent, and with Soviet missiles presenting a permanent clear and present danger to all the European members of NATO, Britain very much included. Churchill's dream, however, was a noble one: to seek to arrange a relationship with Stalin, and those parts of Central Europe under Soviet control, that would make the world a safer and more peaceful place, but without the kind of craven appeasement that he had so staunchly opposed with Hitler in the 1930s.

However, geopolitical realities had changed. The number one world power was not Britain but the United States, and any real role that Britain could now play would be strictly secondary to that of the two post-war superpowers. Churchill thus had all the right intentions, but was alas now far too old-fashioned and living in the great imperial past to understand quite how different things now were.

In this fond illusion Churchill was by no means alone – even in the twenty-first century there are still millions of nostalgic Britons who ascribe to their country a far more important position in world affairs than its size and GDP actually merit. As former Churchill Archivist Correlli Barnett has pointed out in several books, this was not a partisan viewpoint either: Labour Governments continued to pour money into having fleets and armies west of the Suez Canal well into the 1960s, instead of modernizing Britain's archaic factories, labour relations, schools and much else besides. Defeated Germany had an economic miracle; Britain remained decades behind it in all kinds of industrial and similar measurements.

Churchill also kept to his old ways, and his Cabinet contained more members of the House of Lords than any other until over fifty years later in 2009. His wartime personal Chief of Staff General Ismay became, briefly, Secretary of State for Commonwealth Relations, before going on – more appropriately – to head NATO, and Churchill's favourite Field Marshal, Lord Alexander of Tunis, became Minister of Defence. In Downing Street John Colville, one of Churchill's junior Private Secretaries during the war, was recalled to duty as Principal Private Secretary and Churchill's son-in-law Christopher Soames became Parliamentary Private Secretary to the Prime Minister.

The year 1953 saw the coronation of the young Queen Elizabeth II. It was also marked by her making her Prime Minister *Sir* Winston Churchill, since he was awarded the Order of the Garter, Britain's oldest chivalric honour. He had turned down the honour in 1945, since he was still feeling sore at his general election defeat, though he accepted the intellectually superior Order of Merit (that brings huge prestige but no title to its recipients) the following year, 1946. In 1955 he was also to turn down the offer, unique since that conferred on Arthur Wellesley in 1814, of a dukedom, the very highest rank in the British peerage. (Only three subjects have gone from commoner birth to ducal rank, and Churchill, who would have been the fourth, was the grandson of a duke.) This meant that Churchill, while a Knight of the Garter, was still a commoner, and was to die as one, despite his unique and extraordinary service to the nation over six decades.

The coronation year saw Churchill temporarily taking charge of foreign affairs after Eden, who continued to be desperate for the premiership, fell gravely ill when a routine operation was botched and needed to convalesce. Churchill believed in face-to-face summit diplomacy, which had worked for him during the war. But his old confrere, now President, Dwight Eisenhower, on the other hand, did not. An extract from Eisenhower's diary in January 1953 shows this all too well, as well as the sadly diminishing prestige that even Churchill now enjoyed, and the unwisdom of his three circles approach to international affairs:

> Mr Churchill is as charming and interesting as ever, but he is quite definitely showing the effects of passing years. He has fixed in his mind a certain international relationship he is trying to establish – possibly it would be better to say an atmosphere he is trying to create. That is that Britain and the British Commonwealth are not to be treated just as other nations would be treated by the United States in our complicated foreign problems.

In this Churchill has, of course, not been alone – the fanatical desire of Britain's Prime Minister in 2009 to be the first head of government to greet the new President in the White House shows that this is something after which British politicians still hanker.

Eisenhower continued:

> I assured him that I am quite ready to communicate with him personally, on our old basis of intimate friendship, where discussion between us would advance our common interests. But I made it clear to him that when official agreement or understanding must be reached, it must be done through those channels that will establish proper records for the future . . .

On the Europe issue, both Eisenhower and the United States Secretary of State, John Foster Dulles had done all they could to interest Churchill in the new European organization but, as Churchill biographer Geoffrey Best reminds us, these efforts 'got nowhere'. Eisenhower lamented:

> He is unquestionably influenced by old prejudices and instinctive reactions . . . [On Europe it] is almost frustrating to attempt to make Winston see how important it is that . . . [he should exert] leadership in bringing about this development.

Here we have a paradox: an American President doing his best to persuade a British Prime Minister to get more involved in the nascent European Economic Community, yet, five years later, a French President, Charles de Gaulle, would accede to power and use the Anglo-American 'Special Relationship' as his behind-the-scenes excuse to veto Britain from entering the EEC, because the United Kingdom was seen by him as the lap-dog of the United States. That would not have been the case had Britain tried to enter it in 1953, under Churchill, but, as Eisenhower realized, there was no chance that such a thing would happen under someone with Churchill's mindset – one that reflected, it should be said, the old imperial hankerings and nostalgia at the time of the British people. As Eisenhower noticed:

> He talks very animatedly about certain other international problems, especially Egypt and its future. But so far as I can see, he has developed an almost childlike faith that all of the answers are to be found merely in British-American partnership . . . Winston is trying to relive the days of World War II.

It is an *American* President saying this! How many have thought it since? Yet Churchill has almost certainly had most of the British people with him on this ever since.

In 1954 Churchill suffered a catastrophic stroke while hosting a guest from Italy at 10 Downing Street. He was incapacitated for some months, but was able to hide it from even his Cabinet colleagues, in a way that would be inconceivable with a press as intrusive as it is today. 'Rab' Butler, the Chancellor of the Exchequer, Churchill's son-in-law and Parliamentary Private Secretary, and some key Downing Street and Cabinet Office officials were able to maintain a pretence of normality, and the ruse to cover it up clearly succeeded.

But even Churchill could not go on for ever, much though he would have wished to, and although he realized, as he told his Principal Private Secretary John Colville, that he knew his designated successor, Sir Anthony Eden, was simply not up to the task of being Prime Minister. On 5 April 1955 Churchill had a splendid dinner for the Queen at 10 Downing Street, a very rare event, then left the following day. His days of power, half a century after first joining a government as a junior minister at the Colonial Office at the end of 1905, were finally over.

The last decade was not kind to Churchill. The portrait by Graham Sutherland, unveiled in 1954, on his eightieth birthday, while he was still in office, was unflattering, and Clementine secretly destroyed it after his death. His 'Black Dog' depression grew far worse and his ability to combat it with effort and hard work, and the excitement of power, were over. He was still an MP, but not someone who attended his beloved House of Commons that often.

In 1957 his successor Sir Anthony Eden had to resign, in theory over bad health but in practice over the Suez debacle, and Churchill's wisdom was sought on the new leader. Most historians seem to think that Churchill preferred Macmillan, because he had opposed appeasement in the 1930s, to Butler, who though far more experienced, had been a staunch appeaser at Munich and afterwards. One could argue that if this was indeed the case, this was unfair on Butler, who had more political experience, and who was also to miss out on being Prime Minister again in 1963, when Macmillan retired. (Butler had also been a junior minister supporting Indian independence in the 1930s, arguing therefore against Churchill, but there is no record as to whether or not this influenced Churchill's choice a quarter of a century or so later.) But Churchill's views also reflected the prevailing wisdom at the time that Butler lacked the sterner qualities needed for a political leader, something that

Churchill himself evidently possessed, but which his disastrous successor, Eden, had clearly lacked.

In his last years, Churchill spent much time in the sun, and was a guest of the wealthy, including, for instance, the Greek shipping magnate Aristotle Onassis, later famous for marrying President John Kennedy's widow, Jacqueline. He was universally revered, and rightly so, but Eisenhower's acute observations of 1953 were also as true as ever. He was a symbol of bravery and defiance against overwhelming odds, but also of an imperial grandeur that had long since departed, of a nation that was now a decidedly junior partner to the superpower status of his mother's native country, the United States. There, in America, he was and still is revered, perhaps even more so than in his home country, since in the United States he played no part in partisan politics as he did, as Leader of the Conservative Party 1940–55, in the United Kingdom.

On 24 January 1965 he died, and became the first commoner in decades to be accorded the very rare privilege of a state funeral. After lying in state in Westminster Hall (during which I was one of the many to visit it, the kind of event one remembers for a lifetime), the coffin was transported to St Paul's Cathedral for the funeral service, and thence downriver to Waterloo, from where his body was taken to Bladon to be buried in a private family ceremony, near his mother, father and brother, Jack. Most touching of all was the symbolic lowering of the cranes as his coffin passed up the Thames – millions of people around the world were in mourning for the largest than life statesman Britain has produced, certainly for centuries. The American

President, Lyndon Baines Johnson, boycotted the funeral, theoretically because Churchill had not attended Roosevelt's in 1965, but in reality as a snub to the Labour Government of Harold Wilson for not sending British troops to Vietnam. It was a sad reflection on LBJ, as no British Prime Minister had ever been more pro-American than Churchill. And for many in Britain, historians have agreed, Churchill's death really did mark the end of an era.

CONCLUSION

WINSTON CHURCHILL 'WARTS AND ALL'

In his influential essay 'Churchill in 1940: The Worst and Finest Hour', British historian David Reynolds describes his subject at that crucial period:

> . . . recognition of Churchill's remarkable rule in 1940 must be balanced by acknowledgement that he was not always right in his decisions. The old Winston, renowned for his mercurial brilliance, was not banished by new responsibilities. It is a fundamental conclusion . . . that a sober examination of Churchill's performance as war leader in 1940 does not belittle his greatness. On the contrary, it makes him more a human and thereby a more impressive figure than the two-dimensional bull-dog of national mythology. Churchill's greatness is that of a man, not an icon.

This is surely true, not just for the crucial year of 1940 but for Churchill's entire career.

To take the First World War as an example. It is clear that Churchill, as Sir Michael Howard has argued, was responsible for the development of the tank as a weapon of warfare, and was certainly the grandfather of the infant Royal Air Force, if not its actual parent. Both these things transformed the fighting of war not just in the long term but permanently, and Churchill was the genius who saw the potential for both these where many of the hidebound did not. Yet at the same time he micromanaged the Admiralty, including naval operations, and he was the politician above all responsible for the disaster in the Dardanelles (a misjudgement that was to haunt him for decades afterwards), even if others shared much of the blame with him. So in one war we have genius going hand in hand with catastrophe, from the same brilliant but erratic individual.

And the same is true throughout Churchill's life: outstanding insights and towering dynamic leadership, on the one hand, and episodes of reckless folly leading to utter chaos, on the other.

Churchill was always larger than life, so his genius was above that of even the greatest of his contemporaries, but his failures worse than that of a mediocrity.

As noted at the beginning of this book, to write about Churchill is to leap into very dangerous territory, since for many of his admirers the two-dimensional icon *is* Churchill. An icon is by definition a sacred object, something through which to worship divinity, and in an era in which conventional religion is increasingly passé human nature sets up new objects of adoration, whether it is Winston Churchill or his distant relative Princess Diana. Suggest that the idol is even only 99 per cent perfect and the wrath of the devotees will come crashing down upon you!

Thankfully, historians are now trying to look at Churchill 'warts and all' (to use the Oliver Cromwell phrase from the seventeenth century), with both his manifold strengths and regrettable weaknesses, so that we can finally see him as a human being, not as an object of devotion to be worshipped uncritically.

Those for whom any criticism is blasphemy accuse those who disagree with them as 'having an agenda', as if authors never have a purpose in the books they write. And, ironically, to have an agenda or purpose is actually to be profoundly Churchillian, as he was always keen for his books to have, as he would put it, a *theme*.

While for some a statement that Churchill was a mix of genius and blunderer is akin to lese-majesty, what some writers have tried to do in recent years is to achieve *balance*, for the reasons that Reynolds describes so eloquently in the quote at the beginning of this chapter. Hagiography does no one any favours, especially as it acts as the proverbial red rag to a bull, the latter in this case being those historians who love to tear down great names, to discover faults and to make reputations by destroying sacred cows. No one is perfect on the one hand, and no one is always basely motivated on the other. Truth surely lies in a balance of good points with bad, with some, like Churchill, having bad points as the flip side to the coin of the good points that made them so justly famous.

So if this book has an agenda, that is it: to find a balanced way of looking at Winston Churchill, his strengths and weaknesses, his triumphs and disasters, his insights and his blind spots, and then to arrive at a considered view.

So, to take Churchill's idea of a *theme*, what this book has attempted to do is to suggest that Churchill's finest hour was indeed 1940–1, when he really did save Britain from Nazism, and when he also, as Max Hastings has reminded us, saw as no one else did that without the United States, Britain had not a hope of defeating the Third Reich. Whatever his faults – and we should not forget them – this part of the Churchill legend is true, and deserves due prominence.

For all that, though, he was a human being, with human weaknesses, not an icon. And yet the trouble is that to recall this, and to show how it is true, can appear to be dragging a great man down to the level of lesser, less deserving, mortals.

So how can we achieve some balance and a proper perspective? For many, such attempts at balance remain anathema: they can see only their own viewpoint and would disregard any opposing characterizations or attempts to balance their interpretation with others. The result is that a biographer who tries to steer a middle, balanced, course gets attacked from both sides.

So can one say that Churchill was completely morally and strategically right to fight on in 1940, that in doing so he was the saviour of his country – and, at the same time, say that he made many strategic errors during the course of the war, even though his intentions were, of course, always for the very best? That he was right on *the BIG thing*, but that he made plenty of mistakes along the way?

In the Second World War, he was right, for example, in realizing, so unlike most of his colleagues, that

America would come to Britain's rescue, but wrong in disagreeing with his American ally Roosevelt that it would help the war effort considerably if India were given its overdue independence.

Take also the 1930s. Churchill was surely morally and strategically right to oppose appeasement in all its forms, yet profoundly mistaken in spending much of the same decade vigorously opposing even the most limited and restricted forms of decolonization, not to mention his enthusiasm for Edward VIII.

Does such a discussion detract in any way from Churchill's role and reputation as Britain's 'national saviour' in 1940? We are finally getting to a place and time in and at which Churchill can be examined objectively, with his faults fully recognized but his genius and unique achievements fully intact and seen in their proper context.

Take Churchill's interest in small details – what one might well today describe as micromanagement. Much of this was because his fertile mind and imagination meant he was always thinking of new things: as one online Amazon critic put it in a review of a biography of the great man, Churchill was very much a hare in terms of the Greek classical fable of the tortoise and the hare. But his incessant interference, especially during the Second World War, drove his subordinates crazy, especially since many of the endless bombardment of memoranda and questions were in fact irrelevant to the successful prosecution of the war – the Big Picture, if one likes, the domain of the tortoise.

Yet Churchill's creative and questioning intellect and his amazing ability to think outside the box also meant that, just as in the First World War he promoted use of the tank and the Royal Air Force, in the Second World War he was able to bring the brilliant Mulberry Harbour idea (which in fact dated back to the earlier conflict) to fruition in time greatly to aid the success of D-Day.

So his strengths were his weaknesses and vice-versa, and what were sometimes deficits could be, in another context and at another time, pure genius.

That is why it is so important to look at Churchill objectively, as is now beginning at last to happen. While the most draconian revisionist or hagiographer will never be satisfied, most of us will surely realize that to look at Churchill 'warts and all' is still to believe that he was, for all his faults, nevertheless very much the greatest Englishman in history.

BIBLIOGRAPHY AND SOURCES

There are thousands of books written about Winston Churchill, not least the multi-volume official biography begun by Randolph Churchill and finished decades later by Sir Martin Gilbert, all the pre-war volumes also being accompanied by copious companion books containing thousands of letters, telegrams, memoranda and the like. (The wartime correspondence, which is even greater still, will one day be available digitally, though it is not at the time of writing.)

The books listed below, therefore, are only a tiny number of the biographies written on Winston Churchill, and focus particularly on one-volume lives that remain available and that I found particularly helpful in writing this book.

I should make one important point here: since mine is a popular work, not an academic text, I have not given endless footnotes and endnotes. Nor have I endlessly attributed every small point, for example, 'as Richard

Holmes is right to point out' or 'as Piers Brendon shows us once again' – and those that were in my original draft have largely been removed.

With exception of the archive sources noted below, this is a work based mainly upon secondary sources. Scholarly works on Churchill, that quote copiously from original archival material and have numerous endnotes, are listed below and it should, I trust, be obvious to those who have read, or read, these books to see where I have followed the course of, say, the helpful works of Richard Holmes and Geoffrey Best, whose biographies I particularly enjoyed, or the books of John Keegan, Piers Brendon and others who have written first-class lives of Winston Churchill. While it would have been nice to acknowledge all of them in the text, this would have altered the nature of this book, and so I give full tribute to them here. (Paul Johnson's 2009 book on Churchill came out too late for use in this volume.)

One thing also needs to be said: listing a book below does not mean that I would endorse all its contents, but that I found the work helpful in writing my own.

I – Archives

Churchill Archives Centre, Churchill College, Cambridge
George C. Marshall Archives Center Lexington, VA (USA)

II – Winston Churchill: Works Quoted From

Liberalism and the Social Problem (London, 1909)
The People's Rights (London, 1910)
The Second World War: Volume 1: The Gathering Storm (London, 1948)
The Second World War: Volume 6: Triumph and Tragedy (London, 1954)

III – Winston Churchill: General Biographies

Best, Geoffrey, *Churchill: A Study in Greatness* (Oxford, 2003)

Brendon, Piers, *Winston Churchill* (London, 1984)

Charmley, John, *Churchill: The End of Glory* (London, 1993)

D'Este, Carlo, *Warlord: A Life of Churchill at War 1874–1945* (London, 2009)

Gilbert, Martin, *In Search of Churchill: A Historian's Journey* (London, 1994)

Holmes, Richard, *In The Footsteps of Churchill* (London, 2005)

Jenkins, Roy, *Churchill* (London, 2001)

Keegan, John, *Churchill* (London, 2002)

Knight, Nigel, *Churchill: The Greatest Briton Unmasked* (Newton Abbot, 2008)

Moran, Lord, *Churchill: The Struggle for Survival 1940–1965* (Boston, 1966)

Ramsden, John, *Man of the Century: Winston Churchill and his Legend since 1945* (London, 2002)

Rhodes James, Robert *Churchill: A Study in Failure 1900–1939* (London, 1970)

Sandys, Celia, *From Winston with Love and Kisses: The Young Churchill* (London, 1994)

IV – Winston Churchill: Biographies Covering the Second World War

Ambrose, Stephen E., 'Churchill and Eisenhower in the Second World War', in Blake, Robert and Louis, Wm Roger (eds), *Churchill: A Major New Assessment of his Life in Peace and War* (Oxford, 1993)

Catherwood, Christopher, *Winston Churchill: The Flawed Genius of World War II* (New York, 2009)

Charmley, John, *Churchill's Grand Alliance: The Anglo-American Special Relationship 1940–57* (London, 1995)

Grigg, John, *1943: The Victory That Never Was* (London, 1980)

Hastings, Max, *Finest Years: Churchill as Warlord 1940–45* (London, 2009)

Reynolds, David, *In Command of History: Churchill Fighting and Writing the Second World War* (London, 2004)

Reynolds, David, 'Churchill in 1940: The Worst and Finest Hour' in Blake, Robert and Louis, Wm Roger (eds), *Churchill: A Major New Assessment of his Life in Peace and War* (Oxford, 1993)

Roberts, Andrew, *Masters and Commanders: How Roosevelt, Churchill, Marshall and Alanbrooke won the War in the West* (London, 2008)

V – General History

Beevor, Anthony, *D-Day: The Battle for Normandy* (London, 2009)

Ben-Moshe, Tuvia, *Churchill: Strategy and History* (Boulder CO, 1992)

Carley, Michael Jabara, *1939: the Alliance that Never Was and the Coming of World War II* (Chicago, 1999)

Catherwood, Christopher, *Winston's Folly* (London, 2004; US edition: *Churchill's Folly: How Winston Churchill Created Modern Iraq* (New York, 2004))

Davies, Norman, *No Simple Victory: World War II in Europe 1939–1945* (London, 2006)

Gorodetsky, Gabriel, *Grand Delusion: Stalin and the German Invasion of Russia* (New Haven CT and London, 1999)

Herman, Arthur, *Gandhi and Churchill: the Epic Rivalry that Destroyed an Empire and Forged our Age* (New York, 2008)

Hourani, Albert, *A History of the Arab Peoples* (London, 1991)

Howard, Michael *The Continental Commitment: The Dilemma of British Defence Policy in the Era of Two World Wars* (London, 1989)

Karsh, Ephraim and Inari, *Empires of the Sand: The Struggle for Mastery in the Middle East 1789–1923* (Cambridge MA, 1999)

Keynes, John Maynard, *The Economic Consequences of Mr Churchill* (London, 1925)

Manchester, William, *The Last Lion: Winston Spencer Churchill: Alone 1932–1940* (New York, 1989)

Overy, Richard, *Why the Allies Won* (London, 1996)

Pogue, Forrest C., *George C. Marshall: Ordeal and Hope 1939–1942* (New York, 1966)

Pogue, Forrest, *George C. Marshall: Organizer of Victory 1943–1945* (New York, 1973)

Rees, Laurence, *World War II Behind Closed Doors: Stalin, the Nazis and the West* (London, 2008)

Roskill, Stephen, *The War at Sea, 1939–1945* (3 volumes in 4 parts: London, 1954–1961)

Sluglett, Peter, *Britain in Iraq, 1914–1932* (London, 2007)

Storr, Anthony, 'The Man' in Taylor, A.J.P. *et al*, *Churchill: Four Faces and the Man* (London, 1969)

Taylor, Telford, *Munich: The Price of Peace* (New York, 1979)

VI – Interviews

Professor Norman Davies, Oxford University
Professor Richard Holmes, Cranfield University
Professor Paul Kennedy, Yale University
Professor Richard Toye, Exeter University
Professor Geoffrey Williams, INSTEP, Cambridge

INDEX